PRAISE FOR THE
REDUCEDEFFORT® CHANGEOVER SYSTEM

"Ron Heiskell has given the Lean world a gift: an opportunity to improve far beyond what anybody could fathom."

> —*Paul A. Akers, author of* 2 Second Lean, Lean Health, *and* Lean Travel

"We worked with Ron to implement the ReducedEffort process and saw a 30% output improvement after just three days. The real bonus came with the unleashing of employee engagement."

> —*Nick Wilson, President of Morrison Container Handling Solutions; Past Chairman of Packaging Machinery Manufacturers Institute (PMMI); Packaging Hall of Fame inductee*

"Prior to the event, I was viewing this as a repackaged form of SMED. After going through the process, I found it was not that at all. If ReducedEffort is not already the future of changeover improvements, it will be. . . . The process works and is fun at the same time. It makes you think, not just about changeovers but also about so much more that is applicable to operations improvements. I've been through many events and worked with many consultants. Ron is by far the most engaging, interesting, and relevant one. He connects with everyone, and you can't help but learn."

> —*John O., Operations Development Manager, major beverage company*

"This workshop was great. I've been doing this twenty years now and have no problem admitting your process was new to me."

> —*Danny K., Plant Manager, major flexographic printer*

"This ReducedEffort Changeover process absolutely develops standard best-practice work."

> —*Mike S., Technical Manager, major beverage company*

"Ron Heiskell and his ReducedEffort Changeover philosophy has been so successful at our facility because it is highly relatable to the everyday worker and manager. The thought that we can accomplish our goal of changeover-time reduction by shifting our paradigms about how (the manner in which) work tasks are performed versus the speed at which those tasks are performed is both simple and revolutionary."

> —*Tony C., Plant Manager, major beverage company*

"It was the most impactful event I have yet to take part in. ... While you have always taken the stand that it is more about the culture and changing how people view their roles and responsibilities, I never realized just how true it is. I believe your process is key to changing our site's culture, both at the associate level and the management level."

—Dirk C., World Class Manufacturing Lead Consultant, major consumer household products and food manufacturing company

"Every time you come out, you energize a new group and show them what they are capable of and how far they can go to accomplish it. You are truly helping me advance the culture. I love the concept of focusing on effort and effort alone. The big "ah ha" for me is watching how risk and time decrease as effort is reduced."

—Matt R., Plant Manager, major bag manufacturing company

"This training has been impactful in driving out wasted effort. ... The shift in operator thinking has been very exciting and was not fully expected. The presentations and the work during the event were the drivers of this very positive cultural change in the plant."

—John M., Plant Manager, major household cleaning products company

"I just wanted to give you a quick update on our REC progress. The changeover we did this afternoon was 40 minutes. (During the REC Event, the time was reduced from 347 minutes to 108 minutes.) I just wanted to let you know that we continue to make progress! For our plant, the biggest impact from the ReducedEffort Changeover (REC) process was beginning to see a change in culture, where technicians are now engaged in the process and feel some ownership for making the changeover as effortless as possible. Prior to REC, they felt like the changeover was the best it could be, and if it were to be changed, it was management's job to change it. Now, they see they have the ability to make changes."

—Danielle H., Operations Manager, major extruder of plastics

"The REC process provided a fun and very interesting way of engaging all participants to quickly come to time and effort reductions on a changeover for our case packer. I, and I speak for the rest of my plant, have never seen or participated in anything remotely like the training that you gave here. . . . This one will definitely go down in our annals of a worthwhile and fun event. Changeover is one of our biggest losses, and the only way to tackle it or get our hands around it is through your process."

—Doug R., World Class Manufacturing Lead, major food manufacturer

"The plant experienced a forty-three percent and a fifty percent reduction in change-over downtime on their two lines. I'm thrilled to see the huge reductions in change-over times on each line. This process reduces losses, drives up operating efficiency, and makes the operation safer. What a great combination!"

—*Rick M., Director of Manufacturing, major household cleaning products company*

"I can't believe a forty-two–minute filler changeover is now seven minutes. Simply awesome!"

—*Tommy W., World Class Manufacturing Manager, major household cleaning products manufacturer*

"This event was a very positive experience at our plant. As a result, we saw significant reduction and simplification in changeover, plus an increase in operator ownership."

—*Rick V., Plant Manager, major household cleaning products company*

"I participated on the labeler team, and it was impressive to witness how the process really drove results. Prior to the event, a changeover took over seven hundred tasks and sixty minutes to complete. Both of those numbers were cut by fifty percent. The nice thing is that this is not about working harder and faster to achieve a shorter downtime, but rather it is about eliminating wasted efforts. Since the operators were taking charge in figuring out the improved way, you could plainly see their ownership. Very impressive process, and I was grateful to have been a part of it. I firmly believe that this is valuable training and that everyone should go through it."

—*Reyes F., Chemical Engineer, major automotive products company*

"In three days, they cut a changeover downtime from one-hundred-fifty minutes to thirty-five minutes, and we had been doing it the old way for twenty-five years."

—*Dave P., Plant Manager, major plastic bag manufacturer*

"I consider the value of this training to be excellent and priceless due to the excitement and people involvement that it has created."

—*Benvinda S., Industrial Engineer, major vitamin-tablet maker*

"Thank you very much for leading the event this week. We had been working on changeovers here for quite some time and had already made big reductions. For both groups to get an additional fifty percent reduction is really amazing. Doug P. even made the comment that this was the most productive event he had ever participated in since he joined the company twenty-five years ago."

—Jamie O., *Plant Manager, major consumer household products manufacturer*

"I was optimistic that we were going to improve the process, but what impressed me the most is how involved everyone was during the event. You kept everyone interested and involved the entire week. It was interesting to see the shift in attitudes as the week went on. I have had so many positive comments about last week. Everyone is energized and ready to improve even more. Thanks for all your help!"

—Brian V., *Production Manager, major consumer products company*

"Opening people's minds to change is not an easy task. … Your methods are quite effective."

—Vera S., *REC Event participant, major consumer products company*

"A lot of times when involved in a program like this, you lose interest. In this one, you stay interested. You learn how to take ideas and implement them into a change-over in ways you normally wouldn't think of doing."

—Allen B., *REC Event participant, major consumer products company*

"I feel that this event added value to everyone's thinking.and could benefit a number of other lines."

—Jim K., *REC Event participant, major consumer products company*

"I had high hopes for some great results. This training and exercise was better than I imagined."

—Peggy C., *REC Event participant, major consumer products company*

"Great experience. It really changed the way I look at everything."

—Brian P., *REC Event participant, major consumer products company*

"It's what this company needs. . . . I hope we can do the event on other parts of the line."

—Israel M., *REC Event participant, major consumer products company*

"I didn't think we could make the changeover go any faster. . . . [The event] enlightened and empowered us to not just settle on doing things because that's the way they have always been done."

—Rachel V., REC Event participant, major consumer products company

"This event exceeds what I thought was possible."

—Joe L., REC Event participant, major consumer products company

"Being at my first REC Event, I didn't know what to expect, but it was an excellent presentation and overall success. Very rewarding and engaging, and I would participate in another one in a heartbeat. It is an excellent way to see how collaboration with team members can produce good results. Excellent training and presentation."

—Wendy B., REC Event participant, major consumer products company

"The operator's workload became significantly reduced, and the company gained the benefit—a perfect win/win."

—REC Event participant

"Excellent seminar, taught by someone who you can tell has a lot of experience in this field. The ReducedEffort process takes SMED to a totally new level. The results are amazing."

—REC Event participant

"It has been one month since our ReducedEffort Changeover Event, and we had our fourth 'best ever' and smashed our big 'impossible' goal again this week. We have had best ever times four times in the past week. The ReducedEffort process works, and the product output is showing the fruits of this work."

—Rob M., Process Engineer, major ice cream manufacturer

"The event exceeded my expectations, because I did not expect to reduce time while reducing effort. It is amazing what can be accomplished if we change the way we think. This event should be part of any training program, because you can apply these principles to everything we do. This training changed my perspective of looking at things and showed me the true meaning of teamwork. Your class was a wonderful experience."

—Hiram A., Production Supervisor, major bottling company

ReducedEffort® Changeover

ReducedEffort® Changeover

The Lean Way to Quickly Reduce Changeover Downtime

Second Edition

Ron Heiskell

Routledge
Taylor & Francis Group

A PRODUCTIVITY PRESS BOOK

First published 2020

by Routledge

52 Vanderbilt Avenue, New York, NY 10017

and by Routledge

2 Park Square, Milton Park, Abingdon, Oxon, OX14 4RN

Routledge is an imprint of the Taylor & Francis Group, an informa business

© 2020 Ron Heiskell

Library of Congress Cataloging-in-Publication Data

A catalog record for this title has been requested

ISBN: 978-0-367-41571-6 (hbk)

ISBN: 978-0-367-40890-9 (pbk)

ISBN: 978-0-367-81528-8 (ebk)

Typeset in Times New Roman
by codeMantra

To God I give all the glory. "Trust in the Lord with all thine heart; and lean not unto thine own understanding. In all thy ways acknowledge him, and he shall direct thy paths." Proverbs 3:5–6 (KJV)

To Jan, the love of my life, without whom this work would not be possible. I cannot express enough my love and gratitude for all her love, help, support, understanding, and sense of humor throughout the years.

To my children, Jenna and Josh, who have brought and always will bring much happiness to Jan's and my life.

To all the wonderful people who work tirelessly day after day on manufacturing floors throughout the world.

もったいない

Mottainai

"A sense of regret concerning waste when the intrinsic value of an object or resource is not properly utilized"

ReducedEffort®

A Lean strategy to eliminate wasted effort and reduce the time of any process change

ACKNOWLEDGMENTS

Dr. Shigeo Shingo, in memoriam, who showed that machines could be designed to reduce changeover time.

The presidents, vice presidents, and plant managers who allowed me to apply the principles of this book in their manufacturing facilities, and the hundreds of people who have applied the ReducedEffort principles in their work and lives.

Paul Akers, who really gets "it," and who reminded me that "It's not about me" and that we need to give our knowledge to help as many people as possible.

Colleen Sell, my editor, who turned my feeble writing into a book that people could actually understand.

Ana Magno, for her great cover design and layout.

CONTENTS

PREFACE

Hey, Ron, I could have used your help to "reduce my effort" way up here.

—Alan Bean, Astronaut, *Apollo 12*, the fourth man to walk on the moon

In 2017, while on a Lean Tour of Japanese manufacturing plants led by Paul A. Akers, founder and president of FastCap and author of the book *2 Second Lean*, I realized that the Lean-driven continuous-improvement process I had developed in 2005 and had been using for 12 years to reduce changeover downtime on packing machines needed to be revealed to the world. I'd been holding on tightly to my ReducedEffort® Changeover process and making a good living teaching and implementing it at Fortune 500 companies throughout North America. But that trip to Japan inspired me. My objective in developing the process went beyond creating a lucrative career for myself. I wanted to help more people on the plant floor—those dedicated workers who day in and day out conduct changeovers of packaging and processing machines. And working with one company at a time was not getting this incredible process to enough people fast enough.

If you ever visit Japan, you will notice one overwhelming characteristic about the Japanese culture, which Paul Akers brought to our attention on his Japan Study Mission: The Japanese show great respect for people. You see this everywhere—in hotels, restaurants, and manufacturing plants. They value you as a customer, and they value each other.

Assembly-line managers in Japan support ideas that make the assembly of parts easier and simpler. On the Japan Study Mission, we visited Toyota Manufacturing Company, Daiwa House, Isuzu Steel, and Mifune. I was astonished at what I saw. I had read and heard about it for years, but to see it in person literally brought tears to my eyes. It was a beautiful thing to see.

The workers performed their jobs with precise choreographed movements, working at a steady pace. They were not running around trying to fix problems, doing what in America we call "putting out fires." There was no verbal communication between workers because they all knew exactly what to do and when they needed to perform their tasks. Their motions were timed perfectly, and they performed every task smoothly, systematically, and with quality. Quality was built into each task. No rework was required. Everything came off the end of the line without flaws and ready to be delivered to the customer. Because quality was built into each stage of the assembly, no quality check was needed at the end of the line. It was Lean at its finest and a magnificent thing to watch.

I doubt that what I saw on those lines would be considered even remotely possible by most companies in the United States. From what I have seen in U.S. manufacturing plants, workers are living in what Henry David Thoreau described as "quiet desperation." They do difficult jobs like machine changeovers with little or no support from management, which typically shows no concern for making their workers' jobs easier or simpler. Management just wants them to do it faster. When you tell line workers that they need to work faster, all they hear is that you want them to work harder. They are working hard already—too hard, because their tasks are not Lean.

My goal has always been to help the people on the plant floor by reducing their effort—which, in turn, always increases productivity, profitability, and quality—with an end goal of bringing manufacturing back to the United States. To bring manufacturing back to America, the best manufacturing methods must be adopted and practiced.

Ron Heiskell
Managing Member
ReducedEffort, LLC

INTRODUCTION

In one week, this REC Team reduced the changeover time on a labeler from 1 hour–58 minutes to 24 minutes, an 80% reduction.

This is not another book about how to do SMED. Like SMED, ReducedEffort Changeover (REC) does reduce machine-changeover time. But REC is not SMED.

SMED, Single Minute (or digit) Exchange of Dies, developed by Dr. Shigeo Shingo, has been the process used for many years by countless manufacturing plants to reduce the amount of time a machine is shut down to complete a changeover. It took Dr. Shingo nineteen years to develop SMED, and since then, the SMED process has reduced changeover downtime whenever and wherever it has been applied. Product manufacturers, company officers, engineers, technicians, and machine operators around the globe can validate that the SMED system works. Additionally, consumers worldwide have profited by the application of SMED, because when production downtime is reduced, products can be manufactured at lower costs, and lower costs can mean lower retail prices. Dr. Shingo started a manufacturing revolution.

For example, the SMED process was used at a Toyota plant to reduce the changeover of a 1,000-ton stamping press from four hours to three minutes. In 1988, while working at The Clorox Company, I witnessed the changeover of a complete packaging line that had been reduced to 10 minutes as a result of applying the techniques taught in SMED. In 1989, I was a member of a team of engineers at The Clorox Company that applied SMED to a liquid filler, and we reduced the changeover time from six hours to six minutes.

SMED works, it absolutely works, but the SMED process is not a Lean process. Implementing SMED can cost a company thousands of dollars and many months, if not years, and it can be difficult and time-consuming to implement. It can also send the wrong message to the work force, because SMED is focused on reducing time. Reducing the time of the changeover allows the company to produce more product and increase profits; that is the sole purpose of SMED.

Lean is not about making more money for the company, although it inevitably will. Lean is all about improving people's lives and facilitating continuous improvement throughout the manufacturing process. Making the changeover process easier for workers and facilitating continuous improvement throughout the changeover process is the sole focus of the ReducedEffort Changeover system. Reducing effort consequently reduces the time to complete the changeover process (or any process, for that matter). What's more, with the ReducedEffort approach, significant reductions of both effort and time are achieved in one week.

A ReducedEffort Changeover Event is a Kaizen event. The Japanese word *Kaizen* means "change for better" or, as I have heard it defined, "take it apart and make it better." Kaizen can apply to continuous improvement or to a specific event in which change occurs to make something better. A ReducedEffort Kaizen event takes place over five consecutive days, during which the people who do the work (rather than management) "take apart" (analyze) how they've been completing the changeover process and modify that process to "make it better" (easier and simpler).

As a Lean-based process, the ReducedEffort Changeover (REC) system focuses on reducing the labor, not the time, involved in changing over a machine to work on a different product. With REC, there are no Standard Operation Combination Sheets to fill out and no Problem Identification Sheets to complete, and it does not require the arduous chore of timing every task, as SMED does. The REC process has none of those labor-intensive and time-consuming steps. Not using a stopwatch and the absence of charts and graphs may bother many engineers who love that stuff. But to make our workforce Lean, we should be using Lean processes.

SMED is a time-driven process, which means that the changeover tasks that require the most time to complete are generally addressed first. Often these time-consuming tasks are the most difficult and most expensive tasks to address.

REC (pronounced "wreck") is an effort-driven process, meaning that the tasks requiring the most effort are addressed first, regardless of the time required to complete the task. Although all tasks are documented, the time to complete each task is not recorded. The goal is to make the workers' jobs simpler and easier, not to make them work harder and faster. With REC, you don't focus on time at all. You focus on efficiency. But here is the key: As you reduce effort, changeover time automatically decreases.

The bottom line is this: REC, like Lean Manufacturing and Taiichi Ohno's Toyota Production System (TPS), is based on respect for people rather than on company profits. As you simplify people's jobs, the quality of the work increases, safety improves, and the overall time it takes to complete the work decreases. Everyone wins: the workers, management, company, stockholders, and customers.

Unlike SMED—which is complicated, time-consuming, and costly to implement—REC is simple, quick, and low-cost to implement. REC goes after the low-hanging fruit, and it delivers dramatic results in as little as three to five days. To have success in SMED, you must get the changeover down to nine minutes or less, thus the term *single minute*. With REC, any reduction in effort, and subsequently time, is success.

Very little capital investment is required with REC. Unlike SMED, it does not require management-approved funding to achieve substantial results. Typically, results can be achieved with less than $300 in parts. Because REC is not capital-driven, management does not need to drive the process. The operators will drive the process because it reduces their labor. There is something in it for them. One of the biggest advantages of REC over SMED is that operators will readily accept the process, and more important, they will want to sustain it. The reason for this is quite simple and will become evident as you read this book and learn more about the REC process.

Figure 1: Key Differences between SMED and REC

SMED	REC
1. Time-driven process	1. Effort-driven process
2. Weeks/months to implement	2. One-week implementation
3. Results seen over time	3. Immediate results
4. Management commitment	4. Operator commitment
5. Management sees results after large capital investment	5. Management sees results without large capital investment
6. Large capital investment	6. Minimal capital investment
7. Management-driven sustainability	7. Operator-driven sustainability
8. Cultural change not addressed	8. Cultural change integral part of process

While REC is built on the firm foundation laid by Dr. Shingo, REC takes SMED to a new level that is easier and faster both to implement and to deliver sustainable results. To bring manufacturing back to the United States, Lean principles need to be applied in every aspect of manufacturing. Lean eliminates non–value–added tasks.

This book describes the ReducedEffort Changeover system, which I have been implementing, testing, and refining for more than 12 years. It is the culmination of everything I have found to work, all put together in one easy-to-follow package. It explains how anyone can use the ReducedEffort method to reduce both the effort and time it takes to complete their work. Even though the REC process was developed to reduce machine-changeover downtime on the manufacturing floor, it can be applied to any manufacturing process—indeed, to any job—in which a person or a group of people do a series of tasks repeatedly, day after day.

1 THE PROBLEM

In one week, this REC Team reduced the changeover downtime on a case packer by 81%.

When a worker performs a routine operation or process, they typically follow a series of steps that they've acquired through either their previous work experience, instruction from another person who has done the job, or a standard operating procedure (SOP) that was devised by a person or persons with knowledge of what needs to be done to complete the job. Each person, working alone or with other team members, figures out the sequence of performing the tasks that is most comfortable for them, through the scientific method of trial and error. As they repeatedly carry out this sequence of tasks, it becomes more comfortable because they remember what worked well the last time. They continue to build and modify the sequence, and each person's individual way of doing the work evolves. The more times they do the job, the more this sequence is engrained in their mind and becomes their own *paradigm*, or routine, for completing the job. Eventually, workers often reach the point where they believe their way of doing the job is the best or only way to do it.

If the job requires that different people do the same work, such as on different shifts, each person designated to do that job will independently develop their own sequence that is most comfortable for them. If an observer were to closely watch the different people doing this job on different shifts, they would invariably notice that each of the workers perform the sequence differently. What's more, they all believe their way is the best way, because it has become their paradigm.

The reason this occurs is because when a person continually performs a learned activity, a *neural network* develops in their brain. A biological neural network is a string of interconnected *neurons* (brain cells), which when stimulated form a detectible linear pathway in the brain. The more frequently a person does a sequence of tasks in a particular way, the stronger the connections, or *synapses*, between those neurons become. Eventually, after performing a series of tasks repetitively and for an extended period of time, a neural network for that activity is established in the worker's brain, and that activity pattern becomes their paradigm, their set way of doing the work.

Once that paradigm is established, if the person rarely or never varies from that sequence of tasks, regardless of whether others successfully perform the same tasks differently, they have reached what futurist Joel Barker describes as *paradigm paralysis*. Their way is the only way. They literally cannot believe that a more efficient way to do the job is possible. If presented with an alternative way to do the job, they simply reject it because it's not the way they do it.

2 PARADIGMS

In 3 1/2 days, this REC Team reduced the changeover downtime on a case packer by 61%.

Changes in behavior are usually preceded and driven by changes in thoughts and beliefs. So it stands to reason that if you want operators and maintenance mechanics to change the way they do machine changeovers, then the operators and mechanics must first change what occurs between their ears. Yet, far too often the focus is on what operators are doing rather than on what they are thinking. Changing the machine to cause the operators to change the way they work is counterproductive to obtaining sustainable results.

Most operators have their own method of doing changeovers, and even when several people routinely do the same operation in the same facility, each operator typically performs the changeover differently. If you film two different operators doing the changeover on the same machine at two different times and then play both videos simultaneously on two separate TVs, you will notice something interesting. They perform the tasks in different sequences and in different ways. While both operators may successfully complete the changeover, neither way is likely to be the most effective or efficient way to do it. If you ask each of them to explain their method, they will both give rational and logical reasons for their sequential procedures. Typically, they will tell you that nothing is wrong with the way they are doing the changeover. In fact, both of them may tell you that their way is the best way.

Can there be two best ways? Can one best way be agreeable to both operators? The ReducedEffort Changeover process discovers the one best way that is the most effective and efficient method for performing changeovers on any machine.

A consultant could be brought in to watch a changeover and recommend the best way to perform the tasks. But would the operators, who already believe that they are doing it the right way, accept this change? They might do it for a while, but as time goes by, the process will erode and changeover times will creep back up. Adults don't like to be told to change, especially when they have been doing something the same way for many years. Everyone resists change. It is natural to resist change. Why change what has worked in the past? The answer lies in paradigms.

In his video, *The Business of Paradigms*, Joel Barker defines paradigms as "sets of rules and regulations that establish boundaries. These rules and regulations then tell you how to be successful by solving problems within these boundaries."

If you solved a problem in the past by performing a certain set of tasks in a certain sequence, when you are again faced with the same task, you will typically solve it in the same manner. For example, if you have been doing a changeover the same way for the last 10 years, you have established a paradigm—your very own standard operating procedure for that process. As time passes, it becomes increasingly difficult to change that paradigm. Why fix something that isn't broken? The longer you live in your paradigm, the more comfortable you feel in it and the less likely you are to change your way of doing your work. At that point, your paradigm becomes The Paradigm—the only way to do it.

This is a stagnant and unhealthy place for any operator to reside, because if a new paradigm is presented, you will not be able to see that it might be a better way to do it. Your current paradigm will always appear to be the best or only way to do your work. You may assume the new paradigm is wrong or inferior to your method and therefore does not pose a threat to your way of doing things. If you discount this new paradigm as just a feeble or misguided attempt to do it differently, you will resist it or summarily reject it.

New ideas are resisted every minute of every day, often by people who don't want to change because their way of doing something has worked in the past. When you resist a shift in paradigms, you are in a state of paradigm paralysis.

As Joel Barker describes it, "Paradigm paralysis is what occurs when you think that your paradigm is the only way to do something, and paradigm paralysis can blind each one of us to new opportunities and creative solutions to difficult problems"

Paradigm paralysis is not a new or uncommon phenomenon, and it is not restricted to manufacturing. It has existed throughout history, and it occurs in virtually every industry, as the quotes below and elsewhere in the book illustrate.

> "We don't like their sound, and guitar music is on the way out."
>> —*Decca Recording Company, rejecting the Beatles, 1962*

> "Heavier-than-air flying machines are impossible."
>> —*Lord Kelvin, President, Royal Society, 1895*

> "Who the hell wants to hear actors talk?"
>> —*H. M. Warner, Warner Brothers, 1927*

Why would Mr. Warner want to switch to talkies when Warner Brothers and the film industry at large were doing just fine with silent films? Why change when the public was completely satisfied (or so it seemed) with soundless moving pictures dubbed with subtitles and accompanied by music provided by a pianist playing a piano below the screen?

> "There is no reason anyone would want a computer in their home."
>> —*Ken Olson, President/Chairman/Founder, Digital Equipment Corporation, 1977*

> "I think there is a world market for maybe five computers."
>> —*Thomas Watson, Chairman, IBM, 1943*

> "This 'telephone' has too many shortcomings to be seriously considered as a means of communication. The device is inherently of no value to us."
>> —*Western Union internal memo, 1876*

It is certainly understandable that Western Union would find no value in a device that did not use their existing technology. After all, the process of sending a telegram—whereby a keypad operator tapped out a message in Morse code that was transmitted over an electric wire to a distant location, where a telegrapher or a telegraphic machine transcribed the code into a written message—was well established and accepted by everyone. The telegraph system had been a big improvement over the much slower Pony Express mail delivery, and Western Union's profits depended on it continuing.

"The concept is interesting and well-formed, but in order to earn better than a *C*, the idea must be feasible."

> —*A Yale University management professor in response to Fred Smith's term paper proposing reliable overnight delivery service, 1965. Smith later founded Federal Express.*

"Landing and moving about on the moon offers so many serious problems for human beings that it may take science another two hundred years to lick them."

> —Science Digest, *1948. Twenty-one years later, on June 20, 1969,* Apollo 11 *was the first manned spaceflight to land on the moon.*

"While theoretically and technically television may be feasible, commercially and financially I consider it an impossibility, a development of which we need waste little time dreaming."

> —*Lee de Forest, American inventor who helped pioneer sound-on-film motion-picture technology and self-described "father of radio," 1926*

"Television won't matter in your lifetime or mine."

> —*R. S. Lambert, British and Canadian radio broadcaster, 1936*

"The actual building of roads devoted to motor cars is not for the near future, in spite of many rumors to that effect."

> —Harper's Weekly, *1902*

"The ordinary horseless carriage [automobile] is at present a luxury for the wealthy, and although its price will probably fall in the future, it will never, of course, come into as common use as the bicycle."

> —Literary Digest, *1899*

Rail [train] travel at high speed is not possible because passengers, unable to breathe, would die of asphyxia."

> —*Dr. Dionysus Lardner (1793–1859), Professor of Natural Philosophy and Astronomy, University College, London*

"Flight by machines heavier than air is impractical and insignificant, if not utterly impossible."

> —*Simon Newcomb, Director, US Naval Observatory, 1902*

"I can accept the theory of relativity as little as I can accept the existence of atoms and other such dogmas."

> —*Ernst Mach (1838–1916), Austrian physicist*

"X-rays will prove to be a hoax."

—*Lord Kelvin, President, the Royal Society of London, 1895*

"Airplanes are interesting toys but of no military value."

—*Marechal Ferdinand Foch (1851–1929), French general and Supreme Allied Commander during World War I*

"The [flying] machines will eventually be fast. They will be used in sport but they should not be thought of as commercial carriers."

—*Octave Chanute, France-born American civil engineer and aviation pioneer, 1910*

"Fooling around with alternating currents is just a waste of time. Nobody will use it, ever. It's too dangerous. . . . It could kill a man as quick as a bolt of lightning. Direct current is safe."

—*Thomas Edison, American inventor and entrepreneur, ca. 1880*

Isn't it interesting that Edison, who was awarded (singly or jointly) 1,093 patents in the United States during his lifetime, more than any individual in history, was also subject to paradigm paralysis? He heavily invested both his time and money in the generation of direct current. He believed that direct current (DC), not alternating current (AC), should be used to deliver power to the world. He was correct that DC is safer, but his paradigm prevented him from seeing the advantage AC current held in the ability to send power over greater distances. In the end, his paradigm paralysis cost him much wasted time and money.

"A cookie store is a bad idea. Besides, the market research reports say America likes crispy cookies, not soft and chewy cookies like you make."

—*A critic's response to Debbi Fields' idea to start the retail-store chain, Mrs. Fields' Cookies*

"The wireless music box has no imaginable commercial value. Who would pay for a message sent to nobody in particular?"

—*Associates of David Sarnoff at Marconi Wireless Telegraph Company of America (later, RCA) in response to his memo urging the development of a commercial radio receiver for use in the home, ca 1916–1917. In 1920, Sarnoff developed a prototype of his "radio music box" while general manager of RCA.*

"640K [random access memory] ought to be enough for anybody."

—*Bill Gates, Chairman/Founder, Microsoft, 1981*

As amusing as these few examples of the countless quotes reflecting paradigm paralysis may be, they represent the loss of millions of dollars for those who held tight to their paradigm and refused to change. Likewise, refusing to try a different way of doing your job may prevent you from improving the simplicity, ease, speed, efficiency, and quality of your work, and that can result in a missed opportunity to reduce costs and/or increase profits. But when you become so comfortable with a certain way of doing something that it is entrenched, it can be very difficult to change that paradigm even if you are willing to try a different way of doing the work.

Shifting from your paradigm to a new paradigm will never feel right or comfortable. To demonstrate this, please set this book down and fold your arms across your chest. Note which hand is on top. Now, unfold your arms and fold them again but with the other hand on top. Are you able to do it? How does it feel? There is no right or wrong way to fold your arms; whether your left hand or right hand is on top, both orientations work. But you have a preferred way to do it that is comfortable for you. This is your paradigm. Changing your paradigm will always feel awkward and uncomfortable—unless and until you successfully do the new way often enough that it becomes an engrained pattern.

You may ask what all this has to do with changeovers. EVERYTHING! We are asking operators to change the way they have performed their changeovers for a month, a year, or several years. Some may have been doing it the same way for a decade or two decades or even longer. Ask any operator if there is a more efficient way to do changeovers, and they will inevitably tell you that the way they are doing it is the right and ideal way to do it. If their way is the correct and best way, why do two different operators do changeovers differently? Because everyone has paradigm paralysis. Only when people see that a simpler and easier way is possible can paradigm paralysis be overcome.

The REC process allows both managers and operators to quickly see and accept a different way to perform changeovers. Plant managers know how difficult it is to get seasoned operators to change the way they have always performed tasks, such as changeovers. As the REC process is applied, the operators' way of doing changeovers will automatically shift to a new procedure. REC is a systematic approach that guides them through this paradigm shift to quickly accomplish a reduction in downtime losses. The process is simply common sense, but as Voltaire said, "Common sense is not so common."

Manufacturing plants across America are being asked to cut losses everywhere. One of the major loss buckets is the downtime associated with changeovers (the process of changing a machine or line from one product to another). Plant managers, line supervisors, and engineering managers are looking to cut change-over downtime.

When asked, operators will tell you that they are performing the changeovers efficiently and effectively. The fact is, the time of every changeover can be reduced, and it can be reduced within one week. You may wonder how I can make this statement. After all, no one knows the current changeover procedures of every packaging machine (for example) in the country. While this is true, it is also true that operators across the country have typically devised their own methods for changeovers, which are based on the first time they performed the changeover. Over the years their procedures may have evolved, but typically, operators never apply systematic approaches to developing optimized procedures. Even if SMED has been applied to a machine, the time reduction initially realized typically erodes over the years as experienced operators move on to other job functions and new operators are hired.

Figure 2: Actual Results Achieved Using the REC Process

EQUIPMENT	TASK REDUCTION	DOWNTIME REDUCTION
Bag bundler	44%	86%
Bag filler	52%	53%
Bagger / cartoner / case packer	93%	52%
Bag-making machine	89%	80%
Baler	56%	78%
Briquet bagger	59%	74%
Capper	84%	68%
Carton former	50%	54%
Cartoner	47%	58%
Case packer	71%	60%
Cleaner / filler / capper	82%	70%
Film winder	69%	65%
In-line liquid filler	58%	58%
Labeler	28%	26%
Liquid filler	61%	40%
Packer / laner	40%	41%
Rotary filler	41%	33%
Rotary labeler	57%	50%
Rotary liquid filler	45%	73%
Trigger inserter / orienter	48%	59%

Each of these results was achieved within one week and within a budget of less than $300 in parts per machine.

With the hundreds of machines for which I've seen REC applied since 2005, the REC system has never failed to deliver reduced changeover times. For example, one bag-making machine initially had a changeover time of 3.75 hours, and the operators had been performing the changeover the same way for four years. This machine represented the most difficult changeover in their process. After three days of instruction and application of the ReducedEffort Changeover process, the changeover time decreased to 51 minutes, a 77% reduction.

In a joint study conducted by the ARC Advisory Group, Rockwell Automation, and PMMI (Association for Packing and Processing Technologies), it was found that in the food and beverage industry, the average all-inclusive cost of downtime is $7,800 per hour, or $130 per minute. (See Figure 3.) If we assume that this study is correct and use $130 as the minimum, then a 77% reduction in changeover downtime for this bag-making machine equates to a savings of $22,620 every time a changeover is performed. As a more conservative estimate, if the cost of downtime were reduced to $32.50 per minute, the savings would be $5,655 per changeover. Using this more conservative estimate, if this machine were changed over once a month, the savings would be $67,860 per year.

Figure 3: Hourly Cost of Downtime

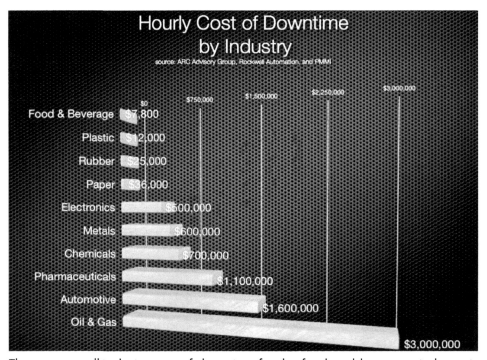

The average all-inclusive cost of downtime for the food and beverage industry is $7,800 per hour.

> Calculating the true cost of downtime at your facility can be very difficult. If you would like to learn an easy way to do this, please see Appendix I.

American industry typically has no idea how much money can be saved by simply reducing the changeover time of just one machine, especially when that machine is the bottleneck, or slowest changeover machine, on the packaging line.

The ReducedEffort Changeover system finds the biggest hang-ups and hiccups in the process—not only in the machine but also and more importantly in the operators' procedures. Even though most operators believe they are performing the changeovers in the most efficient way, if they could actually see a more effective and efficient way of doing changeovers, they would do it. The challenge, as explained in this book, is that paradigm paralysis blinds them to the possibility of a different method that is simpler and easier, especially if they have been doing the job the same way for many years.

> Recommendation: At the start of the ReducedEffort Changeover Event, show Joel Barker's video *The Business of Paradigms* (Original Version), which can be purchased online at Star Thrower Distribution. This video will help to prepare everyone for the paradigm shift that will occur during the REC Event.

3 THE LEAN MENTALITY

In one week, this REC Team reduced the changeover down-time on a filler/capper by 58%.

I f you are in the manufacturing business and have, for example, a packaging line, you might think that the most difficult thing to do is to reduce the change-over time from one product to another. With the prevalent thinking on reducing changeover time in the United States, you are correct. However, there is an "all-

American" process in which multiple tasks are quickly and efficiently performed that many changeover practitioners cite as an example of what can be accomplished when the principles of Lean are applied. I'm talking, of course, about NASCAR and INDY pit stops.

NASCAR and INDY pit stops were super "lean" before Lean became a time-reducing practice of world class manufacturing

When a car pulls into the pit of a racetrack, many jobs need to be performed with spit-second accuracy. The crew jacks up the car, pops the lug nuts, pulls the tires, mounts the tires, tightens the lug nuts, drops the car, runs to the other side of the car, jacks up the car, pops the lug nuts, pulls the tires, mounts the tires, tightens the lug nuts, and drops the car while they also fuel the car and make any necessary chassis adjustments. They do all of this in less time than it took you to read these steps. I have studied pit stops in slow motion and counted every step of the pit stop as a task. What I found was that the average pit stop requires seven men to complete 50 tasks in 11–13 seconds.

Pit stops were not always done at this speed. In the 1950s, pit stops took approximately 4 minutes. What happened to cause the average pit-stop time to change from 4 minutes to 13 seconds—and subsequently to make pit stops deserving of study?

In 1965, the Wood brothers decided to try something new at the Indy 500. That 500-mile race had pit stops that normally would have taken a total of 200–250 seconds to complete. With their "something new," the Wood brothers' crew performed both pit stops in a total off-track time of 40 seconds. Jimmy Clark, their driver, won that race, which changed the way all future pit stops would be performed.

What the Wood brothers did, for the first time in history, was choreograph the pit stop. The reason this had such an impact on the outcome of the race is that at 180 miles per hour, .06 seconds equals one car length on the track. They knew that if they could cut time out of the pit stop, they could win the race. Through choreography and practice, they found and perfected a more efficient way for the pit crew to perform their tasks, reducing their moves and thereby the time it took to complete their tasks.

This changed the way everyone thought about the pit stop and had done pit stops since the inception of racing. Joel Barker describes this as a paradigm shift, where pit-stop crews went from one way of doing the job to an entirely different way of doing it. When this happens, everything goes back to zero. Pit stops could never again be performed the same way they had always been done in the past. The paradigm was shifted forever.

What we now know as the Lean mentality has been applied to pit stops since 1965, and as a result, the changeover has been reduced by 99%. The REC system uses many of the techniques used by race teams.

The 50 tasks performed in 13 seconds in a NASCAR pit stop is equivalent to 13,846 tasks per hour. If you divide that by seven men, that equates to 1,978 tasks per man per hour. This is a shocking number, and no one could maintain that performance for an hour, much less for hours at a time. In documenting packaging-machine changeovers, I typically see 500 tasks per hour performed by each person, or about a quarter of the number of tasks performed by a NASCAR pit-crew member. The American manufacturing community is at least 50 years behind NASCAR and INDY racing teams. What would a pit crew think as they watched, for example, a machine changeover in your facility? They wouldn't believe it. They would be shocked by the wasted motion, the repeated tasks, and the constant walking around the machine to perform the tasks. They would be stunned to learn that the Lean mentality, which is essentially the approach pit crews have been using since 1965, has not yet been applied in U.S. manufacturing.

It doesn't matter how large a company is or how much money they have to throw at the problem of making the work more efficient, I see the same thing everywhere. Very few people are performing their work efficiently. The exceptions to this are the workers for companies that really understand and have adopted the Toyota Production System (TPS). The Toyota Manufacturing plant, the Daiwa House, Isuzu Steel, and Mifune in Japan are great examples of TPS, or Lean manufacturing. Based on my experience, it would be impossible for Mifune to do their 300 to 440 changeovers per day without the application of Lean manufacturing. The workers at these plants move with the choreographed precision of a NASCAR pit crew. The difference is that a pit crew works with choreographed precision for 15 seconds, while the workers in these Japanese plants do it for an entire shift. It is an amazing thing to watch, and if you ever get a chance to go to Japan, I highly recommend that you visit those four plants.

4 THE LEAN APPROACH TO ZERO DEFECT

In one week, this REC Team reduced the changeover downtime on an ice-cream filler by 56%.

In the United States, Lean typically has not been applied to manufacturing processes in which one or more individuals perform a series of tasks to complete a job. The common definition of Lean is simply the practice of searching out all production activities that do not create value for the end user and so are considered waste, and then eliminating those wasteful activities.

At this point, I would like to tell a story that may seem unrelated to the application of Lean, but please bear with me. I think you will see how the story is relative.

Many years ago, I was a drummer with hard-rock bands. One of the negatives of being a drummer is that you are always breaking drumsticks. Do you know the average life of a drumstick in the hands of a hard-rock drummer? Forty-five minutes. Sometimes, a stick breaks the first time you hit the edge of a cymbal or do a rim shot (the tip of the stick hits the drum head at the same time the neck of the stick hits the metal edge of the drum). Other times, they last hours or just whittle down over time before breaking. The reason for this inconsistency of stick life is

That's me in the 1970s.

that they are made of wood, typically oak or hickory. Every stick is unique because each tree and each area of the tree from which drumsticks are made has a different grain structure.

After breaking countless sticks, I began to wonder, *What if they were made out of a different material, one that had the playing qualities but not the grain structure of wood.* I thought there had to be a better way. So I set out to make a synthetic stick that felt and played like wood but would last longer.

Other synthetic sticks had been developed, but all of them had failed. They didn't feel right in a drummer's hand or produce the right sound on the drum. This is another example of paradigm paralysis. If a synthetic stick didn't feel and play like a wooden stick, drummers simply rejected it. I suspect that those synthetic sticks had been developed by engineers rather than drummers. As an engineer and a drummer, an unusual combination, I was determined to make the first synthetic drumstick that felt and played like wood.

After almost three years of trial and error, I had what I thought was it. Now it was time to see what other drummers thought of it. I looked in the local newspaper and saw that the Oak Ridge Boys were playing that night at the Circle Star Theater in San Carlos, California, which was very close to where I lived. I started calling the hotels in the area and asking to speak with Fred Satterfield, the Oak Ridge Boy's drummer at the time. I heard "Never heard of him," "He's not staying here," "Nope, not on our reservation list," and then finally, "Sure, I'll put you through." I told Fred that I was a drummer, that I'd developed a new drumstick, and that I'd like to get his opinion of it. He said, "Come on over to the hotel. I'll introduce you to the boys and take a look at your sticks." So I gathered up several pairs of my sticks, which no drummer but me had seen until then, and drove to the hotel.

Fred liked what he saw and said he would use them in the concert that night. He then asked me how many tickets to the show I would like. I said two, one for me and one for—no, not my wife—but for but for a friend, Jim Stewart, who worked for a production company. I called Jim and asked him if he could get one of the

GREAT STICKS, RON
thanx,

Fred Satterfield, Grammy-winning drummer for the Oak Ridge Boys

professional cameras for the night and that if he could, I would put him on the stage with the Oak Ridge Boys to film Fred using my stick. He said "Sure, see you there."

Jim filmed the concert. Afterward, he also filmed my interview with Fred, in which Fred said, "I can honestly say the balance of the Hi-Skill sticks is the best I've ever felt. I'm really surprised it has taken this long for someone to come up with a stick that felt like wood but would last longer."

Oorah! It was time to show my stick to other drummers. I went to the Cow Palace in South San Francisco and knocked on the stage door. The door opened, and a bouncer asked me what I wanted. I told him I was a drummer and that I had a new kind of drumstick that I would like to show to John Panozzo, the drummer for Styx. He said, "Hold on, I'll be right back." He returned with a stage pass and directed me to the Styx dressing room. John liked them and started using them.

I'll never forget the Styx concert a few weeks later at the Oakland Coliseum, where I saw him drumming with the sticks I'd given him. He liked them enough to continue using them, and after many concerts and regular practices, they hadn't broken. I always say that the feeling that came over me when I saw drummers like Fred and John using my sticks was about the closest a guy could get to how a mother feels when she delivers her baby. You work so hard, and then you see the fruition of your work, and the feeling is difficult to put into words.

I gave my sticks to many drummers to test. Here is what some of them had to say.

"They are durable, matched, and balanced well. I like them."

—*David Garibaldi, drummer for Tower of Power, inductee into the Percussive Art Society Hall of Fame*

"The Hi-Skill sticks allow me to play with confidence because of their durability and superior balance. They sound good on drums and cymbals."

—*Mike Stephans, drummer for Paul Williams, Cal Tjader, Cher, Shirley MacLaine, and David Bowie*

"Best synthetic sticks I have ever played."

—*Ed Shaughnessy, drummer for* The Tonight Show Starring Johnny Carson

"They are the Hercules of sticks."

—*Mingo Lewis, Santana*

Touchdown! I was going to make my drumsticks and make a fortune, or at least a good living, for the rest of my life—or so I thought. One day I loaded the inventory I had into a truck, drove to the local landfill, and watched bulldozers bury all those drumsticks. Can you guess why? No, I hadn't neglected to get an issued patent. No, they didn't break. No, someone else didn't copy them. No, they didn't stop selling. Give up? I closed this business and destroyed my inventory for one major reason: I didn't know who my customer was.

That bears repeating: I didn't know who my customer was. I thought my customer was the drummer. Boy, was I wrong. My customers were the music stores where drummers bought their drumsticks. Drummers loved my sticks, but music stores hated them because they lasted too long. Music stores wanted drummers to break their sticks every week so they would come into the store to buy more sticks and typically buy something else, too. At that time, in the mid-1970s, the internet didn't exist. There was no way to sell directly to drummers. So I went out of business.

It took me years before I could talk about this, but I learned two big lessons about achieving success with an innovative product:

1. Know who your customer is.
2. Know what your customer's requirements are.

The reason I'm telling you this is because this experience later caused me to modify the definition of Lean. I believe Lean should be defined as a production practice of searching out all activities that do not create value for your customer and for your customer's customer, throughout the entire supply chain, to the end user, and then eliminating those wasted activities. This helped me to understand that every person and activity that is downstream at one particular place on a packaging line is a customer of the previous people and activities on the line. Just as drummers weren't the only customer for my sticks, in manufacturing the customer isn't only the end user of the product. There are many customers throughout the supply chain, and all of those customer's needs must be met. If this concept is not understood, then world class manufacturing will never be realized.

World class manufacturers practice Lean throughout their facility, through their suppliers' facilities, and with everyone who handles the component products in the entire supply chain. Zero defects is the standard, not the exception. This is why it's important to build excellent relationships with suppliers. This is an integral element of Lean, yet few companies apply it.

In a 2016 interview with Paul Akers, Ritsuo Shingo (Shigeo Shingo's son) stated, "Before coming to your plant, you should ask your supplier to assure quality. Catch the defect at the supplier. Tell your supplier what quality you expect and to not ship anything that is not quality. Upstream control is better than downstream control."

Out-of-spec parts should never be sent to downstream customers. This is a major problem I have seen at every packaging line I have visited in the United States. The machine operators are constantly adjusting their machines to accommodate out-of-spec parts.

For example, a filler-capper mono-block is receiving bottles from one supplier and caps from another supplier. The filler-capper is set up by the operators to run in-spec bottles and caps. When out-of-spec caps come to the machine, the bottles start missing caps because the caps are getting stuck in the cap chute. This inevitably causes a machine shut-down. The operator then adjusts the cap chute so that the caps will be delivered to the bottles. What the operator has done is adjust the cap chute for out-of-spec caps. That works fine until in-spec caps are delivered to the cap hopper, which requires another adjustment of the cap chute and can cause another shut-down. This downtime is not the operator's or the machine's fault. The operator's job is to produce as many capped bottles at the machine as he can. So he is constantly monitoring the machine's performance and making adjustments to keep the machine running.

This has become so commonplace in U.S. manufacturing that the primary focus of an operator's job is to make machine adjustments to keep the machine running. This is all wasted time and effort. This is not Lean, and it is certainly not world class manufacturing. However, operators live with this reality day in and day out.

Lean is when the operators do not need to make any adjustments to the machine to accommodate for out-of-spec parts. No out-of-spec parts should be delivered to the production floor. In fact, they should not be delivered anywhere at all.

The supplier needs to know what product variation can be tolerated by the machine without having to make machine adjustments. All parts that require machine adjustments must be rejected by the supplier. This requires a partnership with suppliers that is uncommon in the United States but common in Japan.

Mifune of Japan is a supplier to Toyota. They supply 100 million parts to Toyota every year, only 35 of which will have defects. A defect at Mifune can be as small as a scratch on a steel part that will later be powder coated. You may ask why a scratch would be considered a defect when it is going to be covered in paint.

As Ritsuo Shingo states, "Quality is both visible and invisible. A defect is a defect, whether it is visible or invisible. That is the training. If management people tell the workers the defect is not visible so just pass it, people will think that is acceptable and they can sell other [defective] products. *No!* Quality is the key to survive; otherwise, sustainability is not possible."

Quality is both visible and invisible. That thinking has knocked the socks off auto manufacturers in the United States.

Lean is a wonderful idea that is helping businesses throughout the world. It is not a flavor of the month that will fade away, like Six Sigma and other quality-improvement techniques that have been tried and discarded by many major corporations. Lean is here to stay. I believe that if a company doesn't adopt Lean, the company will fade away, overrun by those practicing Lean. Just look at what happened with U.S. automakers after Toyota developed the Toyota Production System (TPS).

Workers adopting the Lean mentality is a critical factor in solving the problem of eliminating non-value–added tasks and movements. As of May 2017, Mifune had one employee who has worked for 827 consecutive days without producing one defect. At 250 working days per year, that equates to 3.3 years without a defect. Remember, at Mifune a scratch on a part is considered a defect even though the part will be powder coated. Imagine how wonderful it would be to be a customer of Mifune. This kind of relationship doesn't just happen. It occurs when everyone in the entire supply chain applies the Lean principles of everyone eliminating waste, everywhere and every day.

5 EMPOWERMENT

In one week, this REC Team reduced the changeover down-time on a plastic extruder by 75%.

Empowerment is one of the most important aspects, if not *the* most important aspect, of the Lean process. That is why meeting with management to discuss the importance of empowering the REC Team to make decisions and to make changes is an essential part of the Reduced-Effort process. (See Chapter 7, Step 2: Prepare for the REC Event.)

Empowerment on the plant floor is a new concept for most workers. Usually, the people who do the work have never been empowered to change how the work is done, and yet they are the changeovers experts. In the plants where I have conducted ReducedEffort Changeover Events, there is a hierarchal chain of command that prohibits the plant-floor experts from making decisions on their own. If you do not empower your people to make decisions that directly affect their jobs, you will never achieve Lean manufacturing.

Without empowerment, the genius of your employees will never be realized. Of the eight wastes (over-production, over-processing, excess inventory, defects, transportation, wasted motion, waiting time, and unused employee genius) listed by Paul Akers in his book *2 Second Lean*, he states that "unused employee genius is the greatest offender." I totally agree.

I have literally turned down work from companies who refused to empower their workers during the one-week REC Event. An executive at one company said, "Sure, we empower our people. They just have to ask permission before making a change." That is not empowerment! The idea of letting the people on the plant floor make changes without management approval threatens many managers and engineers. Yet, the only way to implement Lean is to empower your people.

One engineer at a U.S. Toyota plant told me that when he came to the assembly line one day, he noticed a new platform at a certain location on the line, which wasn't there the day before. He asked one of the line operators where it came from, and he was informed that they were having trouble reaching a certain area on the line, so they took it upon themselves to build and install the platform. They did this to reduce the wasted time and effort to reach something. The Toyota engineer could have attacked them for doing this without asking permission, but he didn't. Instead, he praised them.

Toyota and other Lean manufacturers understand that they hire assemblers not only to do the work but also to think and to improve the process. If the company just wanted the work performed, they could buy robots and turn out the lights. Robots can do the tasks, but robots can't figure out how to improve the process.

The doors on all Toyotas come off the vehicle after it has been painted and travel on a separate conveyor to meet up with the vehicle after all the interior work has been completed. This was not designed into the assembly line by the engineers. The workers came up with this idea because they realized they were wasting much time and effort walking around the doors, opening the doors, and closing the doors. In that case, although the workers came up with the idea of removing the doors, they did not design and build the door conveyor, nor did they install the new system. It took the talents of many people of different disciplines to implement this change, which eliminated much waste from the process.

Empowerment is not anarchy, where people run off and do things without discussing their ideas with others. It is a collaborative effort in which many people get together and talk openly about what needs to be done. Then, they do it with management's full support. It is not the job of management to approve or disapprove of their employees' ideas. The job of management is to bring the resources together to implement the line operators' ideas.

Empowerment of people is *not:*

- Absence or denial of any authority

- Absence of order
- Having responsibility without authority

The three characteristics listed above describe *anarchy*, where everyone does what they want without regard to any authority. Empowerment is not anarchy.

Empowerment is:

- The shifting of authority from management to the people who do the work
- The establishment of an orderly process for change
- Having the responsibility to plan how to work and the authority to carry it out
- The ability to get the right things done without asking permission
- The management of people by results, leaving them free to figure out how to produce those results

Organizations won't thrive and won't survive for long unless every bright mind is engaged both individually and in teams. Empowerment is essential to employee motivation, engagement, and performance, which makes work more productive, satisfying, and enjoyable. Empowerment is also fundamental to the principles of the ReducedEffort Changeover system. The fact is, with authority and freedom come accountability and productivity. Empowerment means managing people by results and leaving them free, within certain boundaries, to figure out how to best produce those results.

Often, the ideas of plant workers are ignored because they have not achieved the educational level of many of their up-line managers. Some managers discount a line worker's ideas simply because they don't have a college degree or may never have finished high school. There is little, if any, relationship between education and genius.

Albert Einstein said, "The only thing that interferes with my learning is my education. . . . It is a miracle that curiosity survives formal education." Einstein was a high school drop-out.

Many other brilliant people who have shaped our world never finished high school, including: John D. Rockefeller Sr. (first recorded billionaire), Henry Ford (founder of Ford Motor Company and inventor of the assembly line), Walt Disney (founder of Disneyland and winner of 22 Oscars for animated motion pictures), Abraham Lincoln (sixteenth President of the United States), Dave Thomas (founder of Wendy's Restaurant), Andrew Carnegie (philanthropist, who gave away more than $350 million during the last 18 years of his life), Colonel Sanders (founder of Kentucky Fried Chicken), George Eastman (inventor of roll film and founder of the Eastman Kodak Company), Thomas Edison (inventor of the incandescent light bulb and the phonograph), Henry J. Kaiser (the father of American shipbuilding, founder of Kaiser Steel and Kaiser Aluminum), Ray Kroc (founder of McDonald's), David Karp (founder of Tumblr, who at age 15 sold his company to Yahoo for $1.1 billion), Richard Branson (CEO of Virgin Airlines), Vidal Sassoon (hair stylist, who at his death was worth $130 million), and many more.

Likewise, there is little, if any, relationship between education and innovation. It rarely, if ever, factors into the generation of an idea whose time has come. The educational level of an individual does not define that individual. Managers: do not underestimate the genius and innovativeness of your employees. To do so is waste. You may already have the resources on your plant floor to propel your company to the next level. There could be untapped ideas in the minds of your employees that can pave the way to world-class manufacturing.

Mitch Zirkle attended one of the first REC Events I conducted. He caught my attention because he wore a T-shirt that read Disgruntled Employee of the Month. After the event, he sent me a note that included the following statement:

> Being a production worker for years meant that I knew exactly what I was doing, and no hot shot PhD from corporate was going to come in and tell me how to do my job. On the first day, Ron asked me how I felt about the event so far. My natural response to him was "Bull- - - -!"

I see this attitude on manufacturing floors far too often. Many operators are tired of the endless parade of new programs with their numerous rules and regulations that management forces them to implement. The rules of the program should never become more important than the needs of the operators. Two of the five steps of 5S (a Lean manufacturing method for organizing a workplace) are "to sort" and "to set in order," but the needs of the workforce should not be ignored when applying those steps. Remember my definition of Lean? Lean is the elimination of all wasted activities—those that do not add value to everyone in the entire supply chain. The people who do the work on the plant floor are in the supply chain.

At one plant I worked with, the employees told me that, due to the implementation of Lean, they were allowed only one waste can for an area on the line. They had to pick where this can was to be located so that the floor could be marked to indicate where the can would always be. However, having the can in one place on the line meant that they would need to make too many trips from the line to the can. This caused them to work harder during the day, and it increased the time required to do their work. These operators figured out a way to not break any rules and still

Problem solved!

reduce their effort. They simply put the waste can on a wheeled platform and placed the yellow location tape on the platform. Then, they could roll the can to where it was needed without breaking any rules.

Most operators on the plant floor, whom I call the experts, are innovative people capable of solving many problems in ways that will increase productivity. We engineers and managers just need to turn those workers loose on the right problems. The operators should not be using their creativity to figure out ways to work around rules and regulations that make it harder to do their jobs.

Back to Mitch Zirkle. Mitch Zirkle was a machine operator on a packaging line. What few people knew was that he had a fabrication shop in his garage at home, where he built cars. During the REC Event, many ideas were generated by the team, and Mitch would convert each idea to a part that could be mounted on the machine. Every day, he would go home and fabricate the parts, and then bring them to the event the next day.

By the end of the REC event, Mitch had this to say:

> The operators in any given plant, in my opinion, know the machines better than anyone. They are, after all, the ones who have to deal with the equip-
>
> ment forty-plus hours a week. Ron has developed an ingenious way of bringing them together and putting their sometimes unheard ideas into action. This, combined with best practices/procedures developed by the operators themselves, provide for immediate results that everyone will be happy with. It is continuous improvement at its best. The empowerment that operators feel after doing a REC Event puts them into a whole new world of opportunity.

Mitch Zirkle, holding innovative parts he made in his garage to test on the machine at the REC Event

> Like Ron said, "Why would anyone not want to make their job easier?"
>
> Ron, thank you for the doors that you have opened for me. Watching the change in our employees and the growth that they have initiated has been one hell of a journey, and it just keeps getting better.

Two years after that REC Event, Mitch found himself conducting REC Events and saw changeovers go from 4–5 hours to as little as 20 minutes. He was no longer operating one machine on a line; he was now increasing productivity throughout the plant and making people's jobs simpler and easier.

During the one-week REC Event, participants are empowered to make any change to the machine or the process without having to ask permission from anyone. Without empowerment, nothing will change. When you empower your "experts" on the plant floor, you will witness amazing results.

6 REDUCEDEFFORT CHANGEOVER: THE REC SYSTEM

In four days, this REC Team reduced the changeover down-time of a filler/capper by 73%.

Many companies hire staff to conduct SMED events to reduce changeover downtime. However, one problem with SMED is that it doesn't address a person's mentality regarding their work. SMED is focused on reducing the time of the changeover. In fact, you haven't achieved success with SMED until you achieve a changeover time of less than 10 minutes, thus the name single minute (or digit) exchange of dies. When you focus on reducing the time, you bypass the most important element of Lean: the way people think about their work. Consequently, SMED doesn't address the paradigm paralysis that every employee has regarding their work.

When I developed the ReducedEffort Changeover system, I focused on changing the way people think about their work, because if you can change the way people think about their work, the way they work automatically changes. I call this Lean mentality. You may ask why a person would be willing to change the way they do their work when they may have been doing it the same way for 25 years or more. The reason is that everyone wants to work less for the same or more pay. If you tell a person that the company needs to cut costs by increasing productivity, they hear that you want them to work harder and faster for the same pay. That does not motivate people to change the way they have always performed their work. However, if you show them how they can reduce their effort and still complete their work, they are interested.

The founding principle of the ReducedEffort method is that if you can reduce the effort of a job, the time to complete the job will automatically decrease. The goal is not to reduce the time; the goal is to reduce the effort.

To prove this concept, I decided to attack a universal problem in manufacturing: the changeover downtime of machines. I had a three-part goal:

1. Solve a problem shared by the majority of manufacturing companies.
2. Solve it very quickly, in one week or less.
3. Deliver dramatic results that were not achievable with any existing process, including SMED.

As a mechanical engineer working with people on production lines, I observed people working very hard to perform the tasks required to do changeovers. It occurred to me that there were simpler ways to accomplish these tasks, but these ways were not obvious to the people doing the tasks. They didn't see the tasks as simple or hard; they just saw the tasks as what they had to do to get the job done. There needed to be a way to reveal to people how much simpler their work could be.

So I started working on a method to expose these difficult tasks. I recognized that I couldn't just walk up to them and tell them how it could be done easier. They wouldn't listen, because how could I, an outsider who had never done those tasks, know a better way to do them. The ideas on how to reduce their labor needed to come from the workers who did the tasks. If the ideas came from them, then they would own the change and be more willing to implement it.

Then, while teaching university classes on product innovation, I discovered why people are unable to see different ways of accomplishing their work. It is because most people see their work from only their point of view. In order to discover innovative ways to perform their work differently, people need to watch themselves from a different vantage point. In the classroom, when people watched a video of themselves performing a series of tasks, they started to see what they'd overlooked before and easier ways to do their work.

It occurred to me that if people in the manufacturing environment could view their work from different vantage points, they, too, could see innovative solutions to things that had bothered them for years and find ways to make their work easier.

This inspired me to video-record the changeover operators doing their tasks and to then play back the video to them. That was the beginning of the REC system.

The benefit of video-recording the changeover is not to document the time required to do each task. In fact, the time it takes to do the tasks is unimportant. The benefit of the video is realized when the operators watch themselves do their work. It is then, and only then, that they come up with innovative ideas to reduce their work.

As I continued to test the REC system, I witnessed the process reducing the changeover downtime every time it was applied. But I still had to perform the ultimate test to absolutely prove its validity: test it on a machine for which SMED had already been applied. If the REC process could reduce the changeover time of a machine where SMED had been applied, then it could reduce the changeover time of any machine. That opportunity came when I was asked to reduce the changeover downtime of a liquid filler. The filler was in a plant where SMED had been practiced for over twenty years. SMED had been applied to this filler with great success, and the plant personnel had continued to make improvements over the years. None of the operators believed that my process could cut any additional time from the changeover. It was a perfect opportunity for the ultimate test.

After only four days of applying the REC system, the changeover time was reduced by 33%. One of the changeover operators commented, "The REC process made us see inconveniences as losses, and it made the work easier." This proved the validity of the REC system and demonstrated that it was filling a gap that wasn't being addressed with SMED.

The key difference was that the REC system focused on reducing the effort, not the time, as SMED does. By focusing on reducing effort, issues that were never addressed when the focus was reducing time came to the surface. The operators who did the changeover on this liquid filler never saw their inconveniences as anything but annoyances or irritations. They didn't see these irritations as unnecessary motions and steps—as wasted effort. The REC system brought to light these wasteful motions and steps, and it provided a platform for addressing these irritations and for implementing unique solutions to eliminate them.

As a result, these innovative ideas to eliminate irritations inevitably reduce the time required to complete the tasks. This is what I call "turning bummers into bucks." When the operator's irritations are eliminated, the production lines have less downtime, thereby increasing uptime and productivity. The ReducedEffort process finds those things that irritate people while they do their work, with the ultimate goal of eliminating those irritations to dramatically decrease the time to complete their work.

Operators who do changeovers usually just live day after day with things that bug them. This is not an isolated problem but rather a universal problem, and operators typically succumb to the realization that their work is tedious and difficult and they can do nothing about it.

Applying the ReducedEffort system to changeovers reveals the irritating, repetitive, and often hard-to-do tasks, and then it examines and simplifies them. After conducting hundreds of REC Events throughout North America, I have seen that when the tasks that irritate people are reduced, their jobs become easier. In addition, the time it takes to do their work decreases, the quality of their work increases, and their work becomes safer. It is a win-win. The company wins due to the increased productivity, and the employees win because their work becomes simpler and easier.

The remaining chapters of this book describe how to use the ReducedEffort Changeover system to achieve a dramatic reduction in downtime in one week. As you read, keep in mind that the ReducedEffort method can be used to quickly and substantially reduce both the effort and the time of any process that involves a series of tasks performed by one or more people.

7 THE REC EVENT

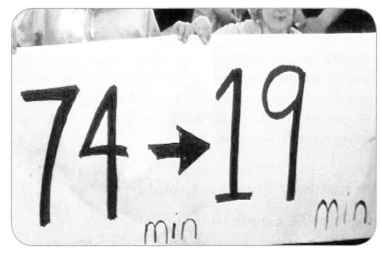

In one week, this REC Team reduced the changeover down-time on a carton former by 74%.

This chapter provides instructions for setting up and conducting a ReducedEffort Changeover Event. You will recognize a few of the steps in the REC process as elements of SMED.

The eight steps to ReducedEffort changeovers are:

Step 1: Video-Record the Changeover

Step 2: Prepare for the REC Event

Step 3: Watch, List, Draw, and Brainstorm

Step 4: Prioritize and Implement Ideas

Step 5: Move and Trash

Step 6: Choreograph

Step 7: Build the Timeline

Step 8: Test, Debrief, and Retest

The Lean coordinator at your facility typically coordinates the ReducedEffort Event to deliver a Lean standard operating procedure (SOP). The REC Coordinator will need to discuss all of the steps described in this chapter and follow them exactly as I have outlined in this chapter. If you are the REC Coordinator, you may have the urge to exercise your innovation skills and change some of these steps. I highly recommend that you don't do that. Each item must be followed exactly as written to guarantee the success of the ReducedEffort Changeover Event.

Step 1: Video-Record The Changeover

Each REC Event focuses on a particular changeover on a specific machine. That changeover must be recorded on video in advance of the event, as the REC Team will watch the video during the REC process. If the changeover requires two or more operators, you will need to make a video of each operator. Video-recording the changeover involves the following steps.

1-A. Select the changeover to be video-recorded.

Responsibility: REC Coordinator

Pick the machine that is the bottleneck on the line, the one that requires the most amount of time to change over. The REC process requires that only one machine be done at a time. This could be, for example, a mono-block filler/capper since that is essentially one machine.

1-B Select the Changeover Expert(s) to be featured in the video.

Responsibility: REC Coordinator

The best changeover operator(s) for that machine—that is, the person or persons (if the changeover requires two or more operators) with the shortest changeover downtime—should "star" in the video.

1-C Line up a videographer.

Responsibility:
REC Coordinator

If the changeover is performed by two Changeover Experts, you will need two cameras and two videographers (one for each Changeover Expert).

Use one video camera per changeover operator.

Contact the camera operator of your choice to discuss the scope of the project and potential dates for recording the changeover. Confirm that person's ability, interest, and availability to do the job. You do not need to hire a professional videographer to video-record the changeover. Just choose someone who has experience operating a camera and knows not to make rapid camera movements.

1-D Schedule the video-recording of the changeover.

Responsibility: REC Coordinator

The changeover that is video-recorded must be an actual changeover, not a simulation of a changeover. So the video must be recorded during normal hours of operation.

To schedule the video, complete the following activities.

1. Consult with the production-line scheduler to determine the day and approximate time to film the changeover.

2. Contact the camera operator to confirm that person's availability. Keep in mind that he or she will need time to set up the camera equipment before the changeover begins and to pack up the equipment afterward.

3. Work out any scheduling conflicts with the production-line scheduler and the videographer.

4. Confirm the day and timeline of the scheduled videotaping with both the production line scheduler and the videographer.

1-E Give the camera operator instructions for recording the changeover.

Responsibility: REC Coordinator

Before the day of filming, meet with the camera operator to discuss the requirements for video-recording the changeover. The meeting may also include the changeover operator(s), if available. This conference must take place before the scheduled date of the videotaping in order to give the videographer time to prepare and test the camera equipment. During the meeting, go over the following instructions and confirm the camera operator's understanding of all these requirements.

Instructions for the Camera Operator

✓ Record the entire changeover of the machine to be analyzed during the ReducedEffort Changeover (REC) Event. This will require multiple camera batteries or a long extension cord.

✓ If the machine requires two changeover operators, use two cameras, one on each operator.

✓ Use a monopod (one-legged stand) for the camera. A monopod prevents the camera operator from pushing "record" on the camera, facing it at the machine, and walking away. A monopod can also be useful in lifting the camera above the operators' heads to look down on what they are doing.

✓ Stay with the camera at all times. Do not turn on the camera and leave the building. (That is exactly what happens if you use a tripod [three-legged camera stand].)

✓ To capture the start time of the shutdown period, point the camera at a clock on the wall or at your watch.

✓ Video-record the operator(s), not the machine.

✓ Make sure to video-record at a distance that shows the operator's upper torso. Do not zoom in so close that you can see only the operator's hands.

✓ Follow the operator(s)'s movements. The video needs to show the operator traveling around the machine as he or she does the changeover.

✓ Follow the operator wherever he goes—for example, if he walks to get parts or tools, to go on break or to lunch, etc.

✓ Do not shut off the video camera until the changeover is complete. However, if the operator leaves the machine to go on break or to lunch, capture the start time of the break and then turn off the camera. At the completion of the break, turn on the camera and point it at the clock to capture the time the changeover resumes.

✓ At the completion of the shutdown period, point the camera at the clock to capture the finish time of the changeover (and the startup time of production).

1-F   Video-record the changeover.

Responsibility: Camera Operator, Changeover Operators, and REC Coordinator

The REC Coordinator must be present for and oversee the videotaping session, as follows.

1. Confirm that the videographer has brought the necessary camera equipment, including a monopod.

2. Make sure the camera equipment has been properly set up.

3. Have the videographer test the camera to ensure it is operating properly.

4. As the camera operator films the changeover, monitor the videotaping to ensure the entire changeover is properly captured.

5. If, at any time, the camera operator runs out of tape, memory, or battery power, he must yell to the Changeover Operator to stop working until the recording can continue. This will ensure that no task is missed on the recording.

1-G   Play back the video to ensure that the changeover was properly recorded and that the playback equipment works properly.

Responsibility: REC Coordinator

Check the video in a quiet place, any time before the REC Event. It is not necessary to preview the entire video; just check to make sure that all of the video requirements were met (see Step 1-E). The REC Team, including the REC Coordinator, will watch the video in its entirety during the Reduced-Effort Changeover Event.

Step 2: Prepare for the REC Event

After the changeover has been successfully recorded on video, all the prep work that needs to be done to ensure the success of the REC Event can be completed, as follows.

2-A   Schedule the REC Event.

Responsibility: REC Coordinator

Most ReducedEffort Changeover Events require one work week to complete, preferably conducted over five consecutive work days. The REC Event may require more than five days if the current changeover time is greater than three hours. As an example, a changeover that averaged 6.5 hours to complete required a seven-day REC Event.

The time required for the event depends upon the number of tasks needed to accomplish the changeover and the number of people participating in the event. The fewer the people, the longer the event. It also depends on whether one video (changeover performed by one operator) or two videos (changeover performed by two operators) will be watched and evaluated during the REC Event. Although it is impossible to know the exact number of days the REC Event will require, I have never seen it take less than three days or more than seven days to complete.

For scheduling purposes, keep in mind that the changeover used to test the new standard operating procedure at the end of the event must be the same changeover in the videotape. For example, if the machine's changeover for product A to product B was filmed, then that same changeover for product A to product B must also be tested. It must be an apples-to-apples comparison.

To schedule the REC Event, complete the following activities.

1. Coordinate with management and others in the chain of command to plan machine downtime for the REC Event.

2. If the line cannot be down for the entire REC Event, plan for machine downtime during five consecutive work days, as follows:

    Day 2: Less than 1 hour, at the end of the day

    Day 3: Up to 8 hours, but can run when the REC Team is in the conference room

    Day 4: Up to 4 hours

    Day 5: Up to 4 hours

3. Consult with management to schedule the dates of the REC Event.

4. Confirm that the Changeover Expert(s) featured in the video will be available to participate in the event.

2-B   Create a list of participants for the REC Event.

Responsibility: REC Coordinator

At the risk of stating the obvious, the REC Coordinator must participate in the event. A minimum of seven other people should also take part in the event. There is no maximum number of participants; in fact, the more, the better.

All of the participants need to speak the same language. The reason I'm saying this is because I've tried to run events that included a few non-

English–speaking people with their translators present, and it made the job for the coordinator more difficult.

Participant List

✓ The changeover operator(s) in the video-recorded changeover.

   NOTE: Each Changeover Expert(s) in the video(s) must participate in the REC Event. If that person (or both people, if two operators perform the changeover) does not show up, the event must be cancelled and rescheduled.

✓ Other Changeover Experts (operators or mechanics) who have performed changeovers of this machine

✓ Changeover Experts who change over this machine on other shifts

✓ Maintenance mechanic(s)

✓ Engineering managers

✓ Production managers

✓ Line operators

✓ Those responsible for producing and maintaining standard operating procedures (SOPs)

✓ Innovators

✓ Purchasing agent

✓ Office personnel

> REC Event participants who are unfamiliar with the machine, such as purchasing agents and office personnel, often come up with brilliant ideas.

2-C Schedule the room where the REC Event will be held.

Responsibility: REC Coordinator

The REC Event will take place in a large conference room, aside from those times when the REC Team goes to the plant floor to observe or test a changeover.

Choose a conference room with enough wall space to accommodate the Post-Its that will be placed on the walls during the event. Typically, 500 tasks are performed by each Changeover Expert per hour, and each task will be captured on a Post-It. For example, if there are two Changeover Experts and the changeover downtime is three hours, there will 3,000 Post-Its on the walls (2 x 3 x 500). (See task 2-G, Acquire all materials needed for the REC Event.)

2-D   Send invitations to required and desired participants.

Responsibility: REC Coordinator

1.   Write the email invitation. Make sure to include the following information.

   • The dates and times of the REC Event

   • The facility and room in which the REC Event will be held

   • The machine and changeover that will be the focus of the REC Event

   • A request to RSVP the REC Coordinator by a specific date

   • A request to communicate any special dietary needs (lunch, snacks, beverages) to the REC Coordinator by a specific date (in time to acquire those items before the event)

2.   Personalize each invitation and send to the recipients at least two weeks before the REC Event. Keep in mind that not everyone receives or reads emails in a timely manner, so you may have to print and hand-deliver some invitations.

2-E   Discuss employee empowerment with management.

Responsibility: REC Coordinator

This discussion can take place on the phone or in a meeting with individual managers or as a group. However the discussion takes place, the manager(s) involved in the discussion should be at the plant-manager level or above. Make sure each manager:

   • Has a basic understanding of the ReducedEffort process

   • Understands the importance of employee empowerment to the Reduced-Effort process

   • Knows the rules regarding changes to the machine that the REC Team must abide by

   • Agrees that the REC Team is empowered to make changes to the physical machine as well as changes to the changeover process

Remember, the most important element of a successful REC Event is empowerment of the participants. They must be encouraged and allowed by management to try new things and to make changes to the machine. Empowerment means not having to ask permission from anyone.

During the REC Event, it may be necessary to order, receive, and install parts or effort-reducing devices. The REC Team must be empowered to make decisions and to order these components—as long as they adhere to ALL of the following rules:

Changes to the machine must be:

- Simple
- Safe
- Low-cost
- Reversible (If a change doesn't work, it can be undone.)

> I have seen great benefit in inviting the plant manager to the first session of the REC Event, which sends the message to the REC Team that they are empowered. Employees typically have trouble believing this and must hear it from top management.

2-F   Arrange for the equipment needed for the REC Event.

Responsibility: REC Coordinator

Make sure all of the items on the following equipment list will be available and in the conference room before the launch of the ReducedEffort Event.

Equipment List
(See Figure 4.)

✓ Enough chairs and enough tables to accommodate all participants

✓ A projector or playback camera for showing the video of the change-over. No audio is needed when you play back the changeover video.

✓ A wall or screen for projecting

✓ At least one easel stand

✓ A computer. This computer will be used to display presentation material and will be plugged into the room sound system.

✓ A white board (which the conference room may already have)

2-G Acquire all materials needed for the REC Event.

Responsibility: REC Coordinator

Before buying or requisitioning the supplies in the Materials List below, purchase one pad of 3M Super Sticky Post-Its® and test them out on the wall of the conference room where the REC Event will be held. Place several Post-Its on the wall and leave them there for a few hours to see whether they'll remain stuck to the wall. If the Post-Its fall off the wall, you'll need to hang blank sheets of 3M Post-It® Easel Pad (flip chart) paper on the wall when you set up the room for the event, so the Task Poster can then stick the Post-Its to these large sheets of paper during the REC Event.

Materials List

✓ Name tents for participants

✓ Pens for participants

✓ 3M Super Sticky Post-Its

- Use only the Super Sticky Post-Its, which adhere well to wall surfaces. I strongly recommend not using the regular Post-Its, which do not stick well to walls.
- For every hour of changeover, you will need an average of 500 Super Sticky Post-Its for each changeover operator. For example, two operators requiring three hours to do the changeover requires 3,000 Super Sticky Post-Its (2 x 3 x 500 = 3,000).
- Purchase whatever color(s) of Super Sticky Post-Its you want. The color of the Post-Its is not a factor in the REC Event.

✓ One pack (six pads) of 3M Post-It Easel Pads / 25" x 30" / white (unlined)

- These "self-stick" easel-pad sheets have an adhesive strip at the top, which is needed to post the pages of ideas to the wall during the event.
- The easel pads will be used to list the effort-reducing ideas generated by the REC Team during the event. Keep in mind that each easel pad contains 30 sheets.
- Additional easel pads may be needed if the Post-Its fell off the wall when you tested them. In that case, blank easel-pad pages will be hung on the wall so the Post-Its can be displayed on them during the event.

✓ An 8.5" x 11" footprint drawing (overhead view) of the machine in the changeover video

- Either hand-draw the footprint drawing of the machine or plot it from a CAD file.
- The 8.5" x 11" footprint drawing of the machine will be used to create Spaghetti Diagrams during the REC Event.
- Make several copies of the drawing. For every Changeover Expert who is recorded doing the changeover, you will need two copies of the machine footprint.

✓ A large footprint plot of the machine in the changeover video

- This drawing must match the 8.5" x 11" drawing used for the Spaghetti Diagrams, but it must be significantly larger.
- This large footprint drawing of the machine in the video can be hand-drawn on an easel pad or plotted from a CAD file.

NOTE: If you plan to hand-draw the machine's footprint on an easel pad, use a sheet from the 3M Post-It Easel Pad, Landscape Format, 30" x 23.5", white (unlined).

- Title this large footprint drawing "Choreograph Master Drawing."
- The Choreograph Master Drawing will be used during Step 6 (Choreograph) of the REC Event.

✓ Erasable markers
✓ Video: *The Business of Paradigms* (Original Version), by Joel Barker. Purchase online at Star Thrower Distribution.

Each Post-It represents one task. A Changeover Expert can typically do 500 tasks per hour.

Footprint drawing of the machine in the changeover video, for use in creating Spaghetti Diagrams during the REC Event

2-H Arrange for lunch and other refreshments for the REC Team.

Responsibility: REC Coordinator

It is best for the REC Team to eat together in the conference room.

You will need to provide enough food and beverages for all participants for each day of the event, as follows:

- Lunch
- Snacks
- Water and other beverages (such as coffee, tea, sodas, juice)

2-I Set up the conference room.

Responsibility: REC Coordinator

This should be done the evening before or the morning of the event.

To set up the room, complete the following activities:

1. Bring the 8.5" x 11" footprint drawings of the machine and the Choreograph Master Drawing to the room.
2. Arrange the tables in a U-shape, with the opening at the front of the room. The reason for this table arrangement is to facilitate task writing.
3. Arrange the chairs around the tables so that all participants will face the center of the U and each other. This also enables them to see the front of the room.
4. Set up and test the equipment (projector, projection screen, computer, sound system, etc.).
5. Set out the supplies (name tents, pens, Post-Its, easel pads, etc.).
6. Make sure beverages and snacks are set up on a table at the back of the room or to one side of the room, so they are accessible to participants but out of the way of the projection screen (or wall) and event activities.

If the Post-Its would not adhere or stay adhered to the wall when you tested them in Step 2-G, hang blank Post-It Easel Pad sheets on the wall, left to right, where the downtime Post-Its will be placed. Write "Downtime" at the top of the first sheet on the left.

Figure 4: Conference Room Setup

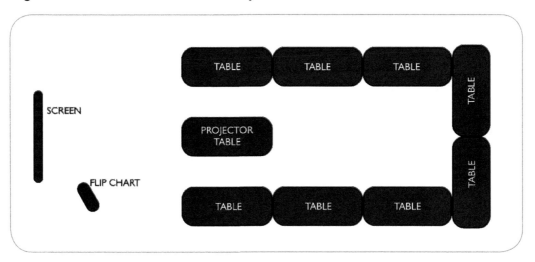

Step 3: Watch, List, Draw, and Brainstorm

The Watch, List, Draw, and Brainstorm process kicks off the REC Event on day one. This vital part of the REC Event can take as few as one day and as many as four days, depending on the overall time of the changeover. Even with an eight-hour changeover, I've never had an event last longer than seven days.

This critical step in the REC process is comprised of the following key activities:

- Watching the video of the changeover
- Writing each changeover task shown in the video on a Super Sticky Post-It
- Placing the Post-Its in sequential order on the Downtime wall
- Creating a Spaghetti Diagram that shows each movement the operator made in the changeover video
- Brainstorming and discussing ideas for reducing the effort of performing the changeover in the video

What Is a Task?

Now is a good time to define what a task is in a Lean process. Better yet, I'd like to show you. So, before you continue reading about how to complete Step 3 (Watch, List, Draw, and Brainstorm) of the REC process, please do this: **Go get a pencil.**

Was that one task? Let's see. . . .

In order to get a pencil, you may have had to:

1. Dog-ear this page (or insert a bookmark) so as not to lose your place.
2. Set the book down.
3. Get up from your chair.
4. Walk to the pencil.
5. Pick up the pencil.
6. Walk back to where you left this book.
7. Sit back down.
8. Pick up this book.
9. Return to the dog-eared (or bookmarked) page.
10. Smooth out the dog-ear (or remove the bookmark).

Ten tasks, not one, just to go get a pencil? Yes!

If, during your REC Event, you were watching a person do these tasks in a video, you would need to write each task on a separate Post-It. You would have used 10 Post-Its just to record the tasks involved in going to get a pencil. I know this may seem ridiculous. But it is vital to the REC process. The value of listing every single task you see in the changeover video will be revealed as you go through the REC process. It can't be by-passed or shortened to reduce the effort of the REC process. This effort is required to reduce the effort of the changeover.

3-A   Assign roles to the participants.

Responsibility: REC Coordinator

Ask for volunteers for the following roles or assign these roles to the people attending the REC Event.

- Changeover Expert(s)
- Coach
- Spaghetti Maker
- Parking Lot Attendant
- Task Writers
- Task Poster

Changeover Expert: This is the operator who was captured on video doing the changeover. As the REC Team watches the video, the Changeover Expert will state the task that is being performed on the screen. The Changeover Expert also operates the computer or camera from which the video is being projected, so he or she must be familiar with the device's play, pause, rewind, and slow-motion (if available) functions. If the changeover requires two operators and two videos were made (one per operator), each Changeover Expert will operate the video-projection device and describe the tasks he or she is performing in his or her video.

Coach: Immediately after the Changeover Expert describes a task, the Coach rephrases the task in as few words as possible, saying it out loud. The Coach makes sure that each task begins with a verb (action word). The Coach also makes sure that each Task Writer knows when to write down their designated task(s).

Task Poster: The Task Poster gathers the Post-Its from the Task Writers after all the changeover tasks in the video have been viewed and written down. This person also numbers the Post-Its in the sequence each task was performed in the video and places all of the Post-Its on the conference-room wall in numerical sequence.

Spaghetti Maker: The Spaghetti Maker creates Spaghetti Diagrams that track the Changeover Expert's movements around the machine and to/from the machine during the changeover.

> Give several copies of the footprint drawing to the Spaghetti Maker. Do this immediately after you've assigned roles, before the REC Event commences.

Parking Lot Attendant: The Parking Lot Attendant stimulates the REC Team to brainstorm and discuss ideas for making the changeover process simpler and easier. He or she writes these ideas on the flip chart. The Parking Lot Attendant should be someone who is willing to challenge existing paradigms (the existing method people use to do things). Typically, the REC Coordinator is the Parking Lot Attendant.

Task Writers: Everyone who has not been assigned a role becomes a Task Writer. As you will see later in the process, some of the mechanics and engineers may need to work on the machine during the REC Event. Therefore, they should take on the role of a Task Writer.

All Task Writers sit around the U-shaped tables. The Task Writers take turns writing the tasks on Post-Its, recording one task at a time, using one Post-It per task, as it is stated by the Coach. The Task Writer makes sure that each written task begins with a verb (action word or phrase), such as "walk to," "turn," "install," "move," "lift," "pick up," etc.

> If the changeover requires two Changeover Experts, there will be two videos, which the REC Team will watch one at a time. After you finish watching the first video, you will repeat the Watch, List, Draw, and Brainstorm process for the second video. In that case: (1) **The Task Poster** places the task Post-Its for the second video on a different wall than the one where the Post-Its for the first video are displayed. (2) **The Spaghetti Maker** makes a separate Spaghetti Diagram for the Changeover Expert in the second video. (3) **The Parking Lot Attendant** makes a separate list of ideas for reducing the efforts of the Changeover Expert in the second video, writing them on a flip chart. He or she then posts the idea pages for video two on a different wall than the one where the idea pages for the first video are displayed.

3-B Complete the Watch, List, Draw, and Brainstorm process.

During this step of the REC Event, all participants watch the video of the changeover as a team. While the video is being watched, the Changeover Expert(s), Coach, Task Writers, Task Poster, Spaghetti-Maker, and Parking Lot Attendant perform their assigned roles, as described below.

REC Team watching the changeover video

Responsibility: Changeover Expert(s)

1. Describe the changeover task.

    a. Explain (out loud) what you are doing in the changeover task as it is plays on the projection screen (or wall).

    b. Pause the video when the task ends, to allow time for the Coach to rephrase the task and for the Task Writer to write it down.

    c. Restart the video after the Task Writer has recorded the task.

2. Pause the video whenever the Parking Lot Attendant or any other participant has a question or idea to share and discuss with the team. When the discussion is over, restart the video and proceed to the next task in the video.

> At first, the process of pausing the video while each task is written on a Post-It will move slowly. As the team becomes more comfortable with the activity, however, the Task Writers will be able to write the tasks as they are called out without the Changeover Expert needing to pause the video. That is why Task Writers stick the Post-Its to their sleeves, from shoulder to wrist. When the process speeds up, this enables the Task Poster to know which Post-Its to pick up from Task Writers first, second, third, and so on and to place them on the wall in the proper sequence.

Responsibility: Coach

1. Rephrase the task in fewer words and always beginning with an action verb, saying it out loud so all participants can hear. This makes it faster and easier for the Task Writers to write the tasks on the Post-Its.

2. If and as necessary, prompt the Task Writer whose turn it is to write down the next task.

Responsibility: Task Writers

The Task Writers take turns writing down the changeover tasks in the video, going clockwise around the U-shaped tables as many times as necessary until all of the tasks have been recorded on Post-Its. I've found the following process to be the most efficient for Task Writers.

1. Write each of your designated tasks on a Super Sticky Post-It, recording the phrase or sentence called out by the Changeover Expert or the Coach, making sure that each task begins with a verb.

2. Repeat the task out loud as you are writing it down.

   This alerts the Task Writer to your left that he or she is next in line to write down a task. It also signals the Changeover Expert that the Task Writer has heard and is writing the task. Additionally, it signals the Parking Lot Attendant or other participants that they can ask a question, share an idea, or initiate a discussion about the task they've just watched.

   If there are no questions, ideas, or discussion, the Changeover Expert resumes playing the video and moves on to the next task in the changeover.

3. Stack the Post-Its on your arm.

   a. Do not put down the pen after writing the task.

   b. With your other hand, tear off the Post-It with the written task from the Post-Its pad and stick in on your shoulder.

      • If you are right-handed, put the Post-It on your right shoulder.

      • If you are left-handed, put the Post-It on your left shoulder.

   c. Stack the Post-Its down your arm, from shoulder to wrist, with the first task at your shoulder.

4. Be ready for your next turn to write a task.

   Keep the pen in your hand and a pad of blank Post-Its in front of you at all times.

Documenting a Task Performed Multiple Times in a Row

When a task involves doing the same thing two or more times in a row, the Task Writer writes down what was done and how many times it was done in the changeover video. For example, if the task required turning a handwheel 15 times, the Task Writer would write the single task "Turn handwheel 15 times" on a Post-It.

However, when numbering the Post-Its on the wall, the Task Poster would count that as 15 tasks. So, if the Post-It for the previous task was numbered 45, the Post-It for the task "Turn hand-wheel 15 times" would be numbered 60 ($45 + 15 = 60$).

Remember, the Post-Its are numbered not only so you'll know where to place them if they fall off the wall, but also so the REC Team can count the total number of tasks performed in the changeover captured on the video.

Figure 5: Task Writer Sequence

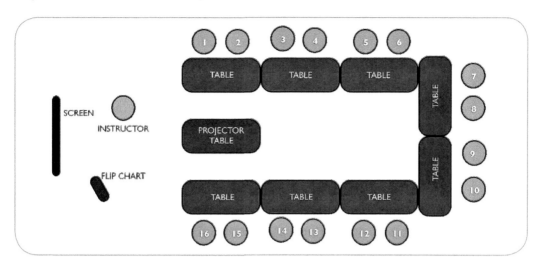

A Task Writer places a Post-It on her shoulder, ready to be picked up by the Task Poster.

Responsibility: Task Poster

While the REC Team watches the video and the Task Writers write the change-over tasks on Post-Its, the Task Poster performs the following activities.

1. Collect one Post-It from each Task Writer.

    a. Go to the person seated at the U-shaped tables who wrote down the first task.

    b. Remove the Post-It from the top of each Task Writer's arm, starting with the person who wrote down the first task and moving clockwise around the U-shaped tables.

    c. Stack the Post-Its in your hand, in the sequence in which the tasks were stated by the Changeover Expert and the Coach.

2. After picking up one Post-It from each of the Task Writers seated at the U-shaped tables, take the Post-Its to the conference-room wall designated for Downtime tasks.

3. Place the Post-Its on the wall in the sequence the tasks were written.
Place the Post-Its left to right, starting the first row as high on the wall as you can reach. After a Post-It has been placed at the end of a row, start the next row on the far left underneath the last row, and continue placing tasks (Post-Its) from left to right.

4. Write the number of each task, starting with the number 1, at the bottom of each Post-It. To make this number more obvious at a glance, you can circle the number on the Post-It.

The reason for numbering each Post-It is two-fold: (1) To determine where the Post-Its go on the wall if some of them fall off during the REC Event, and (2) To determine the total number of changeover tasks captured on the video. Post-Its are not numbered in order to identify the team member who wrote the task.

5. Repeat #1 through #4 (above) until you've collected and attached to the wall all of the Post-Its documenting each task of the changeover.

Task Poster numbering the tasks in the sequence they are performed

Note the circled task numbers on each task.

Responsibility: Spaghetti Maker

1. Draw a line on the 8.5" x 11" footprint drawing whenever the Changeover Expert walks from one point to another during the changeover. (Use a separate footprint drawing for each Changeover Expert.)

These lines are called "moves" on the Spaghetti Diagram.

2. Every time a move (line) is drawn, put a tally mark (hash mark) at the bottom of the drawing.

The tally or hash marks are needed because later it will be impossible to count all the lines, and the team will want to know how many moves the Changeover Expert made during the changeover.

3. Write down the start time of the changeover (as displayed on the clock or watch captured in the video).

4. Write down the finish time of the changeover (as displayed on the clock or watch captured in the video).

5. Calculate the total downtime (from start to finish of changeover), and write it down.

    NOTE: If there are two videos to watch (one for each changeover operator), write down the start time and finish time of each video and determine the overall changeover downtime.

6. Write down the total number of moves for each Changeover Expert, by counting the tally marks.

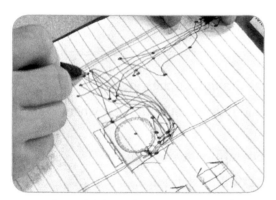 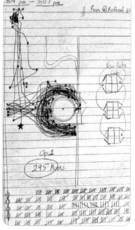

Spaghetti Maker drawing a Spaghetti Diagram of the operator's movements during the changeover

A Spaghetti Diagram, drawn while watching the video, shows the operator's total moves of 295 (tally marks at bottom of diagram). The total changeover time is also captured on the top left of the diagram.

Responsibility: Parking Lot Attendant

This is an important job because this person will continually challenge the changeover process, with the goal of making the job easier.

1. Before the video starts, invite all REC Team members to ask for the video to be paused whenever they want to challenge an existing paradigm. Encourage them to share their ideas on how to make the changeover process easier.

2. Ask "why" and "what if" questions at appropriate times while the video is being watched.

    a. Before posing a question, ask the Changeover Expert to pause the video.

    b. Make sure the focus of your questions is always on how effort can be reduced. Remember, the goal is to make the Changeover Experts' job simpler or easier. For example, "Why is that task done like that?" or "What if we do _____?" or "Would it be easier to do _____?"

> Posing "what if" and "why" questions gets the REC Team thinking about different ways the Changeover Experts can do a task, and they typically prompt short brainstorming sessions. Due to paradigm paralysis, the Changeover Expert will likely defend why he or she is doing a task a certain way. That's okay; it may cause others to engage in the conversation of how to make the job easier.

3. Facilitate the brainstorming of ideas throughout the video.

   Make sure all team members suspend judgement until later, when the idea will be more thoroughly discussed.

4. Document all of the ideas generated during the meeting.

   a. Write each idea on the Parking Lot flip-chart page.

   b. Number each idea sequentially (1, 2, 3, etc.).

   c. When the page is full, flip to the next blank page and continue the sequential numbering of the ideas.

   d. Capture as many ideas as you can without debate.

5. Place the pages of ideas on the Parking Lot wall for all to see.

   a. Make sure each page is numbered.

   b. Tear the pages from the flip-chart pad.

   c. Stick each page to the wall in numerical order.

Parking Lot ideas on flip chart pages attached to the wall

Questions to Stimulate Effort-Reducing Ideas

The following are examples of questions I have asked while viewing changeover videos with REC Teams. Obviously, this is not a complete list, and it won't pertain to every changeover, but these are typical questions that the Parking Lot Attendant can ask during the changeover video to start discussions between team members. What-if questions such as these challenge paradigms and help Changeover Experts recognize easier ways to complete their work.

- What if that tool were mounted on the machine, perhaps with a magnet, so the Changeover Expert would always know where it is?

- What if all those changeover parts were staged closer to the machine, instead of the Changeover Expert having to walk to get them?

- Is there an easier way to do that job?

- What if the Changeover Expert were to use a powered nut-runner instead of a socket wrench?

- What if that handwheel were modified to accept a socket so that a cordless drill could be used to turn the handwheel?

- Does continually locking and unlocking the machine make the Changeover Expert any safer? How can we simplify the LOTO (lockout/tagout) procedure and still meet OSHA requirements and keep our people safe?

- What if a step-stool were placed at the machine location where the Changeover Expert is having a difficult time reaching the machine?

- Why is the Changeover Expert constantly opening and closing the guard doors? Can he do everything that needs to be done at this machine location and then move on, not to return to this location again?

- Would it reduce the Changeover Expert's effort if he or she didn't have to cross over to the other side of the machine?

- What if those parts were color-coded to eliminate confusion as to which parts are needed for each changeover? If that is possible, can a color chart also be mounted on the guard door to show which color is to be used for each product?

- Instead of dealing with infinite adjustments, what if we locate exactly where the positions of the parts are needed, and drill and pin?

- Is there a way to give the Changeover Expert more light so he can better see what he is doing?

Step 4: Prioritize and Implement the Ideas

This step takes place after the Watch, List, Draw, and Brainstorm process has been completed—when all tasks in the changeover video have been written on Post-Its and posted to the Downtime wall, and all ideas for improving the changeover process have been written on flip-chart pages and posted to the Parking Lot wall.

4-A Generate a Prioritized Parking Lot Ideas template.

> ***Responsibility: REC Coordinator***
> 1. Gather all the flip-chart pages on which the Parking Lot ideas were written.
>
>   These ideas will consist of mechanical changes to the machine or changes to the changeover procedures.
> 2. Create the Prioritized Parking Lot Ideas template in your computer.
>
>   This spreadsheet, made with Excel for PC or Numbers for MAC, should include the following columns:
>   - Parking Lot Ideas
>   - Impact on Effort Reduction
>   - Implementation Feasibility
>   - Priority
>   - Responsible Individual and Date
> 3. Type all the ideas on the flip-chart pages in the first column of the spreadsheet. (See Figure 6. Prioritized Parking Lot Ideas). Number each idea as it is numbered on the flip-chart pages.

4-B Prioritize the "parked" ideas, one at a time.

> 1. Project the Prioritized Parking Lot Ideas template on the screen in the conference room so all can see.
>
> ***Responsibility: REC Coordinator***
> 2. Rank the level of impact that the idea will have on reducing effort, using the Priority Key on the Prioritized Parking Lot Ideas template (Figure 6), and add that number (1, 3, or 5) to the template.
>
> ***Responsibility: REC Team***
> 3. Rank the feasibility (level of difficulty) of implementing the idea, using the Priority Key, and add that number (1, 3, or 5) to the Prioritized Parking Lot Ideas template.
>
> ***Responsibility: REC Team***

4. Determine the Priority of an idea, by multiplying its Impact on Effort Reduction rank by its Implementation Feasibility rank.

Responsibility: REC Team

EXAMPLE: If the Impact on Effort Reduction rank is 3 and the Implementation Feasibility rank is 5, the Priority will be 15 (3 x 5).

5. Add the Priority number to the Prioritized Parking Lot Ideas template. This can be easily achieved by building a product equation into the Priority column of the spreadsheet.

Responsibility: REC Coordinator

Figure 6: Prioritized Parking Lot Ideas

Priority Key		Impact on Effort Reduction	Feasibility
1		Little Impact	Difficult
3		Moderate	Moderate
5		High Impact	Very Easy

Parking Lot Ideas	Impact on effort reduction	Feasibility	Priority	Responsible Individual & Date
1. Idea A	1	1	1	Adam xx/xx
2. Idea B	3	5	15	Joe xx/xx
3. Idea C	5	5	25	Mary xx/xx
			0	
			0	

4-C Determine which ideas to implement during the REC Event.

1. Identify the high-priority ideas to be completed during the event.

Responsibility: REC Team

It may not be possible to implement all of the ideas during the week-long event, so some ideas will need to be simulated (when possible). The reason for this is that when the new procedures are tested using the newly implemented ideas and the simulated ideas, you get a time reduction for the changeover. (See Step 8: Test, Debrief, and Retest.) This will then show management that if the simulated ideas were in place, too, the reduced time for the changeover could be equated to increased yearly production.

This makes it very easy to justify to management that a simulated idea should be implemented.

The REC Team must agree on which ideas to implement and which ideas to simulate during the event.

2. On the Prioritized Parking Lot Ideas template, highlight in yellow each idea to be implemented during the event. (See Figure 7.)

Responsibility: REC Coordinator

> It is critical to implement as many ideas as possible during the REC Event. People may tell you it is impossible to implement some of the ideas this week. Resist this negative response, and look for ways to work around the objections to implement the ideas. If an idea absolutely can't be implemented during the REC Event, then devise a way to simulate the idea to test the new SOP. This will demonstrate to your people that the company is completely backing their ideas to make their work easier. Implementing many ideas during the REC Event has a dramatic effect on shifting people out of paradigm paralysis and into the Lean mentality.

4-D   Assign responsibility for implementing each idea during the REC Event.

Responsibility: REC Coordinator

1. Decide which team member is in charge of implementing each idea.
2. Add each person's name to the Prioritized Parking Lot Ideas template.

   Implementing these ideas may require the team member(s) tasked with carrying out the work to order parts or to fabricate parts during the event. That is why I recommend having machinists, engineers, and fabricators on the REC Team. (See Chapter 6.)

4-E   Assign a completion date for each idea to be implemented during the event.

Responsibility: REC Team

1. Discuss the idea with the participant responsible for implementing it, as needed, and come to agreement on a completion date.

2. Add the completion date for implementing each idea to the Prioritized Parking Lot Ideas template.

Figure 7: Implemented Parking Lot Ideas

Priority Key		Impact on Effort Reduction	Feasibility
	1	Little Impact	Difficult
	3	Moderate	Moderate
	5	High Impact	Very Easy

Parking Lot Ideas	Impact on effort reduction	Feasibility	Priority	Responsible Individual & Date
1. Idea A	1	1	1	Adam xx/xx
2. Idea B	3	5	15	Joe xx/xx
3. Idea C	5	5	25	Mary xx/xx
			0	
			0	

4-F. Begin executing the ideas to be implemented during the REC Event.

Responsibility: REC Coordinator

This task is performed when all Parking Lot ideas have been prioritized.

1. Print several copies of the Parking Lot Ideas spreadsheet (the filled-out template), and distribute a copy to each member of the REC Team.

2. Determine whether any parts need to be ordered to implement the ideas. If parts need to be ordered, this is the time to do it. (See Appendix II.)

3. Release the team members who are implementing Parking Lot ideas during the event.

   a. Allow those who can help implement the ideas (mechanics and/or engineers) to leave the conference room and go to the machine. They will start making the changes that the team has agreed can be accomplished during the REC Event.

   b. Ask the mechanics and engineers to come back to the conference room whenever they can to give the REC Team a status report on their progress. Anytime the mechanics and engineers are not busy with the machine on the plant floor, they should return to the conference room to resume their positions as Task Writers.

   c. The Changeover Experts and everyone else must remain in the conference room to continue with the REC process.

Step 5: Move and Trash

This step takes place after the REC Team has decided which Parking Lot ideas will be implemented and tested during the REC Event. The purpose of the Move and Trash exercise is to determine which tasks in the video can be done while the machine is running (moved to uptime) and which tasks are unnecessary and can be eliminated (trashed).

The Move and Trash segment of the REC Event involves the following steps.

5-A Assign roles to the appropriate team members.

Responsibility: REC Coordinator

1. Instruct the Changeover Experts to stand in front of the wall where the Post-Its of tasks performed in the changeover video are displayed.

   For this step, the Changeover Experts are the operator(s) in the video and others familiar with the changeover.

2. Instruct the Changeover Expert(s) in the video(s) to read his or her tasks one at a time in the sequence performed.

   If the changeover requires two operators, Changeover Expert 1 reads all his tasks first, then Changeover Expert 2 reads all his tasks.

3. Instruct a Changeover Expert who is not in the video to transfer task Post-Its from the Downtime wall to the Uptime wall, as needed.

4. Instruct the other participants to stand in a line, single file, extending from the Changeover wall to the Trash wall.

5. Instruct the last person in line to transfer task Post-Its from the Downtime wall to the Trash wall, as needed.

5-B Read the task out loud.

Responsibility: Changeover Expert(s) in the video(s)

1. Find the Post-It for the first or next task you performed in the video.

2. Leave the Post-It on the Downtime wall as you read the task clearly and loudly enough for the whole team to hear it.

   NOTE: If the changeover requires two operators, CE1 reads all tasks he or she performed in the video (one at a time), and then CE2 reads his/her tasks.

5-C   Determine whether to retain, move, or trash the task.

Responsibility: REC Team

Changeover Expert reading each task (Post-It) out loud

1. Based on the changes the team has agreed to make, discuss whether the task can be eliminated or whether it can be done while the machine is running (uptime) rather than when the machine is shut off to complete the changeover (downtime).

   NOTE: Some Parking Lot ideas implemented during the event will be mechanical changes to the machine, and some will be procedural changes to the way the changeover is performed. For example, if the team decided to stage the changeover parts near the machine, then the tasks in the video showing the Changeover Expert walking to get those parts would be moved to the Trash wall.

2. Decide whether to move the task to uptime, trash it, or retain it as part of the downtime changeover process. The team must reach consensus on this decision.

   – If the task can be moved to uptime, continue with Step 5-D.

   – If the task is unnecessary and being trashed, skip Step 5-D, and proceed to Step 5-E.

   – If the task is still part of the downtime changeover process, skip Steps 5-D and 5-E, and proceed to Step 5-F.

   NOTE: If a task will still be done during the changeover, leave that Post-It where it is on the Downtime wall. As task Post-Its are moved to uptime and trashed, there will be gaps between the tasks that remain on the Downtime wall.

5-D   Move the task to the Uptime wall.

Responsibility: Changeover Experts in video(s)

1. Remove the Post-It from the Downtime wall.

2. Place the Post-It on the Uptime wall, in the proper sequence.

3. Proceed to Step 5-F.

5-E   Move the unnecessary task to the Trash wall.

1. Remove the Post-It from the Downtime wall.

   Responsibility: Any Changeover Expert

2. Hand it to the first person in the line of participants assigned to trash unnecessary tasks.

   Responsibility: Any Changeover Expert

A "bucket brigade" of REC Team members transferring unnecessary tasks from the Downtime wall to the Trash wall

3. Pass the Post-It down the line of participants to the person nearest the Trash wall.

   Responsibility: Participants assigned to the Trash-wall bucket brigade

4. Place the Post-It anywhere on the Trash wall.

   Responsibility: Last person in the Trash-wall bucket brigade

> It is very important that the REC Coordinator explain to the Changeover Experts that the tasks are to be analyzed based on the changes to the machine and the changes to the procedures that were agreed upon and documented in the Parking Lot Ideas template. Remind them that if they do the same thing they've always done, nothing will improve. This is an opportunity to try new things to see whether they work. While the Changeover Experts are moving tasks to uptime and trashing tasks (5-D and 5-E), you may need to remind them a couple of times that the agreed-upon Parking Lot Ideas will be implemented this week. The downtime tasks need to reflect these changes.

5-F Repeat Steps 5-B through 5-E until every task in the changeover video has been allocated.

Responsibility: REC Team

Completion of the Move and Trash segment of the REC Event yields the following results:

- Every task that will now be performed during uptime (when the machine is running) is displayed on the Uptime wall, in numerical sequence.

- Every unnecessary task that is being eliminated is displayed on the Trash wall.

- Every task that will still be done in downtime (when the machine is shut down) remains where it was initially placed on the Downtime wall, which now has gaps where the trashed and uptime Post-Its have been removed.

A wall of Trash (no-longer-needed tasks) at the end of the Move & Trash exercise

Only the needed downtime tasks are left on the Downtime wall, leaving gaps where the uptime and trashed tasks have been removed.

Step 6: Choreograph

All previous activities (Steps 1–5) leading up to this point make it possible to complete the most important step in the ReducedEffort Changeover process: choreographing how the changeover operator(s) will perform the new SOP. Like all other steps in the REC process, even though this step is specific to a machine changeover, this choreographing exercise works wherever a series of tasks is performed by one or more people to complete a job.

Isuzu Steel, a supplier to Toyota of Japan, does 48 die changeovers per machine during an eight-hour shift. That's one changeover every ten minutes. They are able to do this because all of their tasks are choreographed.

When I was at Isuzu Steel, I witnessed three people plus one robot load and unload cutting dies with remarkable precision. There was no rushing, and no communication was needed between operators. When it was time for the robot to perform its tasks, music would start playing to let the operators know it was time to back out of the machine and let the robot do its work. When the robot completed its tasks, the music would stop. The music was an audible indicator for the operators to increase their safety. When operators finished their tasks, they would go to another location to help other operators with their tasks until it was time to return to their own station. It was amazing to watch humans, machines, and materials choreographed with precision to achieve optimal quality with safety.

Choreographing the changeover during a REC Event involves the following steps (6-A through 6-F).

6-A On the Choreograph Master Drawing, mark each location where the Change over Expert(s) stopped to do work.

Responsibility: All Changeover Experts, including the operator(s) in the video(s) as well as other team members who are familiar with the changeover process

1. Place the Choreograph Master Drawing and the Spaghetti Diagram side by side on a flat table.

   • The Choreograph Master Drawing was created by the REC Coordinator (Step 2: Prepare for the REC Event).

   • The 8.5" x 11" Spaghetti Diagram showing the operator's moves during the video-recorded changeover was created by the Spaghetti Maker (Step 3: Watch, List, Draw, and Brainstorm).

2. Gather around these two drawings so all the Changeover Experts can see both the Spaghetti Diagram and the Choreograph Master Drawing.

3. Using the Spaghetti Diagram as a guide, mark each location where the operator(s) stopped to do work.

   a. On the Spaghetti Diagram, find each location where the operator stopped to do work and number these "stop" locations (1, 2, 3, etc.). You don't need to number the locations in the order the work is performed; just number them in the sequence each stop location is identified. In other words, don't look for the first place you do work and label that number 1. The numbering sequence is inconsequential.

b. Write down the number of each stop (1, 2, 3, etc.) on the corresponding area of the Choreograph Master Drawing.

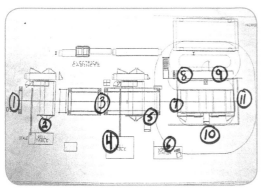

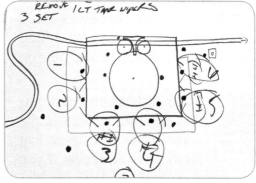

CAD-generated Choreograph Master Drawing, with numbered locations marked

Hand-drawn Choreograph Master Drawing, with numbered locations marked

6-B Create a numbered and labeled flip-chart page for each machine location on the Choreograph Master Drawing.

Responsibility: REC Coordinator

This step is completed after the Changeover Experts have numbered all the work locations on the Choreograph Master Drawing.

1. Go to the flip-chart easel.

2. Write the number of the work location at the top of the page and circle it.

3. Next to this number, write down the name (label) of that location.

4. Flip to the next blank page, and repeat #1 and #2 (above) for the next location.

5. Repeat #1 through #4 (above), until you have numbered and labeled a flip-chart page for each numbered location on the Choreograph Master Drawing.

Flip-chart page showing the location number and location name of the area on the machine where the first downtime changeover task is performed

6-C. Place all of the numbered Loction pages on a blank wall, in the same posi tions they appear on the Choreograph Master Drawing.

Responsibility: REC Team

1. Look at the blank wall as if a footprint drawing (overhead view) of the machine were on the wall.

2. Place each numbered Location page on the wall in the approximate area where that location would appear if you were looking down on the machine from above.

The Location wall, with each numbered Location page positioned in its approximate position on the machine, as identified on the Choreograph Master Drawing

6-D Create a Walk-To page.

Responsibility: REC Coordinator

1. Write "Walk To" at the top of a 3M Post-It Easel Pad (flip-chart) page.

2. Hang the Walk-To page on a different blank wall than the wall displaying the numbered Location pages.

6-E Station the team members at the front of the room.

Responsibility: REC Coordinator

1. Instruct the Changeover Experts to stand in front of the Downtime wall, where the Post-Its for the tasks that are still part of the changeover were left during the Move and Trash segment (Step 5) of the REC Event. These experts include the operator(s) in the video(s) and other team members who are familiar with the changeover.

REC Team members standing in line waiting to receive tasks (Post-Its) for each machine location on the Location wall

2. Assign a team member to hold the Choreograph Master Drawing.

   Instruct this team member to stand close to the Changeover Experts so they can see the drawing.

3. Assign a team member to handle walk-to tasks.

4. Assign a team member to handle uptime and trashed tasks.

5. Instruct the remaining team members to form a single-file line next to the Changeover Experts.

6. Briefly explain the REC Choreograph process to the REC Team. (See Step 6-F: Choreograph the changeover tasks.)

> As the Changeover Experts read and discuss down-time tasks during the Choreograph segment of the REC process, they typically find more downtime tasks that need to be trashed or moved to uptime. They may also need to add new tasks to the downtime change-over process. This is normal and to be expected.

6-F Choreograph the changeover tasks.

The tasks are choreographed, one by one, in the order the task Post-Its appear on the Downtime wall (left to right, top to bottom).

1. Ask a Changeover Expert to read the first task on the Downtime wall.

   Responsibility: REC Coordinator

2. Read the task out loud so all team members can hear.

   Responsibility: Changeover Expert

   – If it is not a walk-to task, continue with #3 (below).

   – If it is a walk-to task, proceed to #11.

Changeover Experts reading the down-time tasks out loud

3. Find the task location on the Choreograph Master Drawing.

Responsibility: Changeover Experts

4. Call out the number of the location where the task is performed.

Responsibility: Changeover Expert who finds the task location on the Choreograph Master Drawing

5. Remove the Post-It for that task from the wall and hand it to the first person in the line of team members.

Responsibility: Changeover Expert who finds the task location on the Choreograph Master Drawing

6. Read the next task on the Downtime wall.

Responsibility: Changeover Expert

Read the task out loud so everyone on the team can hear it.

– <u>If it is not a walk-to task</u>, continue with #7 (below).

– <u>If it is a walk-to task</u>, proceed to #11.

7. Find the task location on the Choreograph Master Drawing.

Responsibility: Changeover Experts

8. Call out the number of the location where the task is performed.

Responsibility: Changeover Expert who finds the task location on the Choreograph Master Drawing.

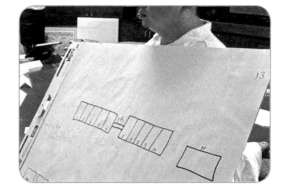

A REC Team member holds the Choreograph Master Drawing, so the Changeover Experts can find the location on the drawing where a task is performed.

– <u>If the task is performed at the same location as the last task</u>, continue with #9 (below).

– <u>If the task is performed at a different location than the last task</u>, proceed to #10.

9. Collect all Post-Its for tasks performed consecutively at that location.

Responsibility: First team member in line

a. Stack the Post-Its in your hand in the order received, with the first one on top of the stack.

b. <u>When a task is called out for a different location than the location on the Post-Its stacked in your hand</u>, continue with #10 (below).

NOTE: When two or more tasks for the same location are called out in a row, the person at the front of the line stays there collecting Post-Its until a task is called out for a different location.

10. Place the task(s) on the corresponding Location page.

REC Team member receiving all tasks (Post-Its) performed consecutively at a particular location on the machine

   Responsibility: First team member in line

   a. Take the Post-It from the Changeover Expert.

   b. Leave the front of the line and walk to the Location wall.

   c. Go to the numbered Location page for the task(s) in your hand (the location number called out by the Changeover Experts).

   d. Place the Post-It(s) on the Location page in sequential order, from left to right.

   e. Return to the end of the line.

11. Place the walk-to task on the Walk To page.

   Responsibility: Team member designated as walk-to task handler

   a. Take the Post-It from the Changeover Expert.

A REC Team member places his stack of Post-Its on the numbered Location page on the Location wall.

   b. Place the Post-It on the Walk To page in the order it was removed from the Downtime wall (see task number on Post-It).

   c. Return to the Downtime wall, and continue with #6 of step 6-F.

12. Repeat #6 through #11 of Step 6-F (Choreograph) until every Post-It has been removed from the Downtime wall and placed on either a numbered Location page on the Location wall or on the Walk-To page.

At that point, all downtime tasks performed at each location on the machine will appear in sequential order on the corresponding Location pages.

> While choreographing the changeover, the Changeover Experts will typically find unnecessary tasks and uptime tasks that were missed during Step 5 (Move and Trash). These need to be moved to the Trash and Uptime walls during Step 6 (Choreograph).

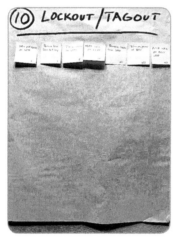

All tasks performed at Location #10

"Walk to" tasks

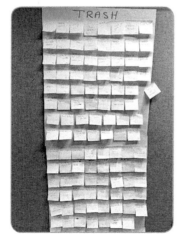

Trashed tasks

Uptime tasks

Keep in mind that uptime tasks are those that can
be performed while the machine is running and making product. Uptime tasks might include, but are not
limited to, bringing change parts to the machine,
repairing change parts, color-coding change parts,
completing any required paperwork, placing change
parts at the point of use, gathering all needed tools,
placing tools at the point of use, staging carts that
hold replacement change parts, staging carts to receive removed change parts, positioning ladders,
getting key and lock for lockout/tagout, etc.

Step 7: Build the Timeline

In this step, the REC Team produces a relative Timeline showing the sequence of
tasks to be performed during the changeover downtime. First, however, the team
must analyze all of the moves made during the changeover to determine whether
more tasks can be done at one location before moving to another location.

During the Timeline-building process, the Changeover Experts may find additional tasks that need to be moved to the Uptime or Trash walls. They may also
need to write additional Post-Its to capture new Downtime or Walk-to tasks that
will be performed in order to implement the Parking Lot ideas.

Remember: Management has agreed that the team is
empowered this week and has the liberty to make any
changes without asking permission to do so.

7-A Designate team members to perform special roles during the timeline process.

Responsibility: REC Coordinator
1. Designate a team member to perform each of the following activities during the timeline exercise:
   a. Bring numbered Location pages to the Timeline wall.

    b. Write new tasks on Post-Its, as requested by the Changeover Expert.

2. Station the Changeover Experts at the Timeline wall.

This is the wall where the Post-Its for existing Downtime tasks were first placed, before the tasks were choreographed (that is, moved to Uptime, Walk To, Trash, or the numbered Location pages).

3. If the changeover in the video has one operator, continue with Step 7-B.

If the changeover already has two operators, skip Step 7-B and proceed to Step 7-C.

7-B Discuss the possibility of using two Changeover Experts for the changeover.

Responsibility: REC Team

1. Study the Spaghetti Diagram to analyze how often and when the operator is moving between the two sides of the machine.

2. Discuss the viability and the potential benefits of performing the changeover with two operators—one on each side of the machine.

3. Decide whether to add a second operator to the changeover process. The REC Team must reach consensus on this decision.

4. If the changeover now uses two operators, continue with Step 7-C.

If the changeover will continue being done by one operator, skip Step 7-C and proceed to Step 7-D.

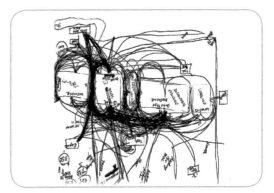

Spaghetti Diagram, showing tasks performed on both sides of the machine by one Changeover Expert

Adding a Changeover Operator: Points to Consider

The REC Team may argue that there aren't enough people on the line to add another person to the machine changeover. The REC Coordinator can make the following points to help get the team thinking about the effort-reduction potential of having two operators do the changeover:

- Ask the team if a Changeover Expert working on a machine downstream from this one can help with the changeover of this machine. Adding a second Changeover Expert would enable this machine to be changed over faster, and then both Changeover Experts could go downstream and work on the second machine.

- Remind them that when the line is down, the company is not making any money. Just like in NASCAR, the longer a car is in the pit, the less likely it is to win the race.

- Point out that moving from one side of the machine to the other is work. The goal is to reduce the work, and one way to do that is to add a second Changeover Expert on the other side of the machine.

- Tell them a synergy occurs between two operators doing a changeover together, which further reduces the overall time of the changeover. This is something I have observed whenever people work simultaneously on opposite sides of the machine. You might think that two operators would reduce the downtime by 50%, but when two operators do the changeover on opposite sides of the machine, I typically see the downtime reduced by 67%, due to the synergy that occurs.

7-C Label the rows where tasks performed by each operator will be placed on the Timeline.

Responsibility: REC Coordinator

1. On the now-empty wall that previously held all Post-Its for downtime tasks performed in the video(s), place four blank Post-Its at the far-left side of the wall—stacking them one below the other in a column, about six inches apart.

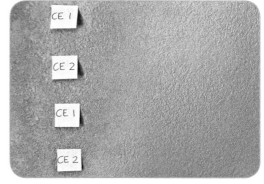

2. Label the first and third Post-Its "CE1" (Changeover Expert #1).

3. Label the second and fourth Post-Its "CE2."

Labels marking the first and second rows of tasks for each Changeover Expert (CE1 and CE2)

7-D Add the first downtime task of the changeover to the Timeline.

1. Determine the area on the machine (location) where the first changeover task is performed.

   Responsibility: REC Coordinator

   a. Ask the Changeover Experts, "Where on the Choreograph Master Drawing do you need to be to start the changeover?"

   b. Call out the number of the location where the changeover begins.

2. Bring the page of downtime tasks for that location to the Timeline wall.

   Responsibility: Team member designated as Location-page mover

   a. Find the numbered flip-chart page for the location called out by the REC Co-ordinator.

   The downtime tasks (Post-Its) performed at this location were placed on the corresponding numbered Location page in Step 6: Choreograph.

   b. Bring the Location page to the Timeline wall, and hold the page so the Changeover Experts can see it.

   Changeover Expert removing a task (Post-It) from the Location page for transfer to the Timeline wall

3. Place the Post-It for the first downtime task of the changeover on the Timeline wall.

   Responsibility: Changeover Expert

   a. Remove the Post-It from the numbered Location page.

   b. If the changeover is performed by two operators, determine whether the first task is done by Changeover Expert #1 or Changeover Expert #2.

   c. Place the Post-It on the Timeline wall, as follows:

      • If the changeover is performed by a single operator, place the Post-It on the top-left of the Timeline wall.

      • If the first task of the changeover is performed by Changeover Expert #1, place the Post-It to the immediate right of the Post-It labeled "CE1."

- If the first task of the changeover is performed by Changeover Expert #2, place the Post-It to the immediate right of the Post-It labeled "CE2."

EXAMPLE: The REC Team decides to add a second changeover operator, and the Changeover Experts determine the changeover starts at Location #10 (E1 Lockout) and is performed by Changeover Expert #1. The Post-It for the first task of the changeover is removed from Location page #10 and placed in the row of tasks for "CE1" on the Timeline wall.

Changeover Expert placing a downtime task (Post-It) on the Timeline wall in the appropriate row for the Changeover Expert who does the task, in the sequence the task is performed at that location

---

While building the Timeline, the REC Team may decide to trash tasks, move tasks to uptime, and/or add new downtime or walk-to tasks. Move the Post-Its for trashed tasks to the Trash wall, and move new uptime tasks to the Uptime wall. For each new Downtime and Walk-to task being added (to implement a Parking Lot idea): Write the task on a Post-It (as directed by the Changeover Expert), and place the new Downtime or Walk-to task on the Timeline in the appropriate sequence and on the appropriate operator's timeline (CE1 or CE2).

7-E. Place all downtime tasks that can be performed consecutively at this location on the Timeline.

Responsibility: Changeover Experts

Complete the following steps for each downtime task that can be performed at this machine location before moving to another location.

1. Remove the next task (Post-It) from the numbered flip-chart page for this location.

Remove Post-Its in the order they are displayed on the Location page—that is, left to right, top row to bottom row.

NOTE: A team member should already have brought the Location page to the Timeline wall. (Sec Step 7-D and Step 7-F.)

2. Determine whether the task can be performed without first completing one or more tasks at a different location.

The goal is to perform all tasks, or as many tasks as possible, at one machine location before moving on to another machine location.

NOTE: If the team wants to change the order of one or more tasks, they can do so at any time during the Timeline build.

- If this task *can* be performed at this location without completing one or more tasks at another location(s), continue with #3 (below).

- If this task *cannot* be performed at this location until one or more other tasks are completed at another location, proceed to Step 7-F.

3. If the changeover will be performed by two operators, decide whether Changeover Expert #1 or Changeover Expert #2 will complete the task.

4. Place the task Post-It on the Timeline wall.

   a. Put the Post-It to the immediate right of the last task placed on the Timeline for that Changeover Expert (CE1 or CE2).

   b. When you reach the end of the first row of tasks for that Changeover Expert, place the next task Post-It at the far left of the second row.

5. If all tasks performed consecutively at this location have been placed on the Timeline, proceed to Step 7-F.

The Changeover Experts will want to do the tasks in the same order they have always, done them, as captured in the video(s). Explain to them that to reduce the effort, the changeover must be done differently. It is extremely important for the Changeover Experts to complete as many tasks as they can in one area before moving to another area. Moving all or most of the tasks from a Location page to the Timeline wall before moving on to another location. It not only forces the Changeover Experts to shift their paradigm, it also reduces the number of moves (effort) required to do the changeover.

7-F   Move on to the next location in the changeover process.

1. Specify the machine location of the next downtime task(s) being added to the Timeline.

    Responsibility: Changeover Experts

    a. Consult the Choreograph Master Drawing and the tasks (Post-Its) on the Location page(s), as necessary, to determine which location the operator must "walk to" to perform the next task(s) in the changeover.

    b. Call out the number of the next location.

2. Add the walk-to task to the Timeline.

    Responsibility: Changeover Expert assigned to this activity

    a. Go to the flip-chart page where walk-to tasks (Post-Its) are displayed.

    b. Find a walk-to task (Post-It) for the machine location where the next task will be performed and remove it from the Location page.

    c. If a walk-to Post-It for that location cannot be found or doesn't exist, have a team member write a new one describing where to walk.

    d. Stick the Walk-to task (Post-It) on the Timeline wall, placing it to the immediate right of the last task placed on the Timeline.

        If two operators perform the changeover, make sure to put the walk-to Post-It on the Timeline for the Changeover Expert (CE1 or CE2) responsible for performing the task(s) at that location.

3. Bring the Location page (of downtime tasks) for the new location to the Timeline wall.

    Responsibility: Team member assigned to this activity

    a. Find the numbered flip-chart page for the location called out by the Changeover Expert.

    b. Bring the Location page to the Timeline wall and hold the page toward the Changeover Experts or attach it to the wall in clear view of the Changeover Experts.

4. Return to Step 7-E, to add the remaining tasks performed consecutively at this location to the Timeline.

    EXAMPLE: The Changeover Experts say they need to "walk to" Location #2 on the Choreograph Master Drawing to complete the next tasks(s) in the changeover. One of the Changeover Experts removes a Post-It that reads "Walk to Location #2" from the flip-chart page containing all walk-to Post-Its (Step 5: Choreograph) and places this walk-to Post-It on the Timeline wall. Meanwhile, the designated team member removes the flip-chart page for Location #2 from the Location wall and brings it to the Timeline wall. The Changeover Expert then removes tasks (Post-Its) that need to be performed at Location #2 from the Location page and places them to the right of the tasks that are already on the Timeline wall.

Changeover Experts have brought the Location page to the Timeline and attached it to the wall.

When completed, the Timeline wall represents the sequence of tasks performed by the Changeover Expert. If two operators are used to do the changeover, there will be two timelines: one for Changeover Expert #1 (CE1) and one for Changeover Expert #2 (CE2). These timelines are the standard operating procedures (SOP) for each operator and indicate when to do their respective work.

Completed Timeline. Note the bump-up, which enables the Team to insert additional Post-Its where needed without having to move all the Post-Its to the right to make room for them.

7-G   Generate new standard operating procedures (SOPs) for the changeover.

Responsibility REC Coordinator

This step is performed when:

- All downtime tasks (Post-Its) on all Location pages have been removed and placed on either the Timeline wall, the Uptime page, or the Trash wall.
- All walk-to tasks (Post-Its) have been either placed on the Timeline wall or trashed.
- Any new tasks have been written on Post-Its and placed on the Timeline wall.

1. Remove all downtime tasks from the Timeline wall.

   Responsibility: REC Coordinator or any team member assigned by the REC Coordinator

   For each Changeover Expert (first CE1, then CE2), do the following:

   a. Pull the downtime Post-Its for that Changeover Expert from the Timeline wall in the sequence the tasks will be performed—left to right, top row and then bottom row.

   b. Stack the Post-Its in your hand, with the first downtime task performed on top and the last downtime task performed on the bottom.

2. Create the new ReducedEffort Downtime standard operating procedure (SOP) for the changeover.

   Responsibility: REC Coordinator

   If two operators perform the changeover, generate a Downtime SOP for each Changeover Expert. (See Figure 8 and Figure 9.)

   a. At the top of the document, type the following information in this sequence:

      • "Operator 1" or "Operator 2" (if two operators perform the changeover)

        NOTE: The term *Operator* can be interchanged with *Changeover Expert*, if you prefer.

      • Production facility and area

      • Changeover ID (product X changed to product Y)

      • "Downtime Tasks"

   b. Type the changeover downtime tasks in the SOP document.

      • List the downtime tasks in the sequence they were on the Timeline wall, using the verbiage on each Post-It.

      • Number the downtime tasks in the order they will be performed.

        NOTE: These numbers will not match the numbers on the Post-Its.

   c. Print two copies of each Downtime SOP (Operator 1 and Operator 2).

3. Remove all uptime tasks from the Uptime wall.

   Responsibility: REC Coordinator or any team member assigned by the REC Coordinator

   For each Changeover Expert (first CE1, then CE2), do the following:

   a. Pull the uptime Post-Its for that Changeover Expert from the Timeline wall in the sequence the tasks are performed—left to right, top row and then bottom row.

b. Stack the uptime Post-Its in your hand, with the first uptime task performed on top and the last uptime task performed on the bottom.

4. Create the new ReducedEffort Uptime standard operating procedure (SOP) for the changeover.

   Responsibility: REC Coordinator

   If the changeover requires two Changeover Experts, generate an Uptime Changeover SOP for each operator.

   a. At the top of the document, type the following information in this sequence:

   - "Operator 1" or "Operator 2" (if two Changeover Experts perform the changeover)
   - Production facility and area
   - Changeover ID (product X changed to product Y)
   - "Uptime Tasks"

   b. Type the uptime tasks in the SOP document.

   - List the tasks in the sequence they appeared on the Uptime wall, using the verbiage on each Post-It. (See Figure 10.)
   - Number the tasks in the order they will be performed.

     NOTE: These numbers will not match the numbers on the Post-Its.

   c. Print two copies of each Uptime SOP (Operator 1 and Operator 2).

5. Review the new Downtime standard operating procedure (SOP).

   a. Project the completed ReducedEffort Changeover Downtime SOP on the screen.

   Responsibility: REC Coordinator

   If there are two SOPs (one per Changeover Expert), project both documents on the screen—side by side, with Operator 1 on the left and Operator 2 on the right.

   b. Read the new Downtime SOP out loud.

   Responsibility: Changeover Expert(s) assigned to perform the test

   If two operators will perform the new Downtime SOP, the two Changeover Experts take turns reading their respective tasks, in increments of 10 tasks each.

EXAMPLE: Changeover Expert 1 reads tasks 1–10 for Operator 1; then Changeover Expert 2 reads tasks 1–10 for Operator 2. Next, Changeover Expert 1 reads tasks 11–20 for Operator 1, followed by Changeover Expert 2 reading tasks 11–20 for Operator 2. This alternating reading continues until the Changeover Experts have read all tasks for Operators 1 and 2.

   c. Identify any needed corrections to each Downtime SOP.

- Discuss the new Downtime SOP to determine whether any downtime tasks need to be rearranged (performed in a different sequence), moved to Uptime, eliminated, or added.

   Responsibility: REC Team, led by the Changeover Experts performing the test

- Make note of all needed corrections to the new Downtime SOP.

   Responsibility: REC Coordinator

> This will be the final review of the SOP prior to going to the floor and testing the tasks. You will typically need to make corrections to the SOP during the SOP-review process. As the Changeover Experts read their respective tasks out loud, have them envision doing the tasks in their minds. I have found that as they mentally picture doing the tasks while they read them out loud, they always rearrange, add, and delete tasks. Don't be surprised by this.

6. Review the new Uptime Standard Operating Procedure (SOP) for the changeover.

   a. Project the completed ReducedEffort Changeover Uptime SOP on the screen.

   Responsibility: REC Coordinator

   If there are two new Uptime SOPs (one for each Changeover Expert), project both documents on the screen—side by side, with Operator 1 on the left and Operator 2 on the right.

   b. Read the new Uptime SOP out loud.

   Responsibility: Changeover Expert(s) assigned to perform the test

   If the Uptime SOP requires two operators, the two Changeover Experts take turns reading their respective tasks, in increments of 10 tasks each.

    c. Identify any needed corrections to the new Uptime procedure.

- Discuss the new SOP to determine whether any Uptime tasks need to be rearranged (performed in a different sequence), moved to Downtime, added, or eliminated.

Responsibility: REC Team, led by the Changeover Expert(s) per forming the test

- Make note of all needed corrections to the new Uptime SOP.

Responsibility: REC Coordinator

7. Update the REC Standard Operating Procedures (SOPs) for the changeover.

Responsibility: REC Coordinator

    a. Make all corrections to each new Downtime SOP document.

    b. Make all corrections to the new Uptime SOP document.

    c. Print two copies each of the new ReducedEffort Downtime and Uptime SOP documents. (See Figures 8, 9, and 10.)

Figure 8: ReducedEffort Changeover Downtime SOP / Changeover Expert #1

DOWNTIME TASKS

Operator: __1__

Line: __XXX__

Product __A__ to Product __B__

1. Walk to west Start-Stop button at door #4.
2. Push stop button.
3. Raise guard door #4.
4. Push start button to prove that guard door interlock is functioning.
5. Walk to Position 1 (to raise height of Marsh printer).
6. Find height adjustment.
7. Turn first handwheel with drill.
8. At Position 2, turn second handwheel with drill north side of Marsh printer.
9. At Position 3, move south side rail to proper position with drill.
10. Walk to door #4.
11. Step up.
12. At Position 4, adjust upper tool compression (hand crank).
13. At Position 5, loosen Kipp handle south side exit rail.
14. Pull rail completely to stop.
15. Tighten Kipp handle.
16. At Position 6, lower compression tool.
17. At Position 7, adjust for tool length (hand crank).
18. Adjust width of lower tools (hand crank).
19. Go to Position 8 for machine height.
20. Adjust machine height with hand drill.

Figure 9: ReducedEffort Changeover Downtime SOP / Changeover Expert #2

DOWNTIME TASKS

Operator: 2

Line: XXX

Product A to Product B

1. Walk to case guide rail adjustment going to palletizer.
2. Lift pin.
3. Pull back case guide.
4. Reinsert pin.
5. Walk to case reject.
6. Loosen two Kipp handles on each rail.
7. Push rail to stop.
8. Tighten two Kipp rails.
9. Loosen two Kipp rails on west rail.
10. Bring rail back to stop.
11. Tighten two Kipp handles at scales.
12. Walk under conveyor with safety plate.
13. Walk to north exit rail.
14. Raise Door #3.
15. Loosen one Kipp handle.
16. Pull rail back to stop.
17. Tighten one Kipp handle.
18. Go to pull pin at glue head.
19. Pull out quick pin.
20. Adjust glue nozzle to proper spot.
21. Replace pin.
22. Close door #3.

Figure 10: ReducedEffort Changeover Uptime SOP

UPTIME TASKS

Line: XXX

Product A to Product B

1. Stage new change parts cart at the point-of-use.
2. Verify that all change parts are in good working order.
3. Repair change parts.
4. Make sure all color-coded change parts are in the correct bin.
5. Complete all changeover paperwork.
6. Gather all needed tools for changeover.
7. Place tools at point-of-use.
8. Place parts at point-of-use.
9. Stage carts to receive removed change parts.
10. Position ladders.
11. Get key and lock for lockout/tagout.
12. Place step stools where needed.

13. Make sure new bottles are ready and in place.
14. Make sure new caps are ready and in place.
15. Clean all change parts.
16. Make sure there are no missing change parts.
17. Notify Quality Assurance when the changeover will begin.
18. Notify Process when the product change will occur.
19. Unroll water hoses and place at point-of-use.
20. Alert the rest of the line when the changeover will occur.
21. Put on any required protective clothing.
22. Verify that Changeover Experts are in place and ready to begin.

The Uptime SOP is not necessarily in sequential order. The Changeover Experts can decide who will do each uptime task, evenly distributing the work to themselves or others.

Step 8: Test, Debrief, and Retest

This last segment of the ReducedEffort Changeover Event involves the following activities:

- Testing the new Uptime and Downtime standard operating procedures (SOPs) by performing the changeover on the machine in real time, on the factory floor

- Discussing the results of the tests and making improvements to the SOPs

- Retesting the revised SOPs by performing the changeover on the machine

- Generating the final ReducedEffort standard operating procedures for both the Uptime and Downtime changeover processes

The following guidelines for the Test, Debrief, and Retest process assumes that two operators perform the changeover.

8-A Designate the team members who will participate in the testing and retesting exercises.

Responsibility: REC Coordinator

1. Assign the following roles to the appropriate individuals.

Changeover Expert: The operator(s) who performed the changeover in the video and/or other operators on the REC Team who have performed the changeover in the past.

Coach: One per Changeover Expert

Spaghetti Maker: One per Changeover Expert. Typically, any team member who performed this task while watching the video also does it during this test of the new SOP.

Timekeeper: Any team member can be assigned to perform this task. The REC Coordinator should also record the time as a backup to the Timekeeper.

Because the Changeover Experts have not yet memorized the new SOP, their assigned Coach reads the tasks out loud to the Changeover Experts who perform the changeover test. The Coaches should be familiar with the changeover process, so they will know when a task is nearing its completion and when it's time to call out the next task.

2. Hand out the following materials.

- SOP documents for Operator 1 and Operator 2—to the respective Coaches
- Two copies of the 8.5" x 11" footprint drawing of the machine—to each of the Spaghetti Makers
- A small notepad—to the Timekeeper
- Clipboards—one to each of the Coaches and Spaghetti Makers
- Pens—to the Spaghetti Makers, the Timekeeper, and other team members (for taking notes)
- A digital camera that captures both still photographs and short videos— to the REC Coordinator

8-B Complete the Uptime tasks.

Responsibility: Changeover Experts

The changeover's Uptime tasks must be completed according to the new Uptime SOP prior to testing the new Downtime SOP.

8-C Test the Downtime standard operating procedures (SOPs).

Responsibility: REC Test Team—which includes the designated Changeover Expert(s), one Coach for each Changeover Expert, one Spaghetti Maker for each Changeover Expert, the Timekeeper, and the REC Coordinator

Keep in mind that for each Changeover Expert performing the changeover, a Coach and a Spaghetti Maker are required. Only one Timekeeper is required because only the overall time of the changeover (and not the time of each Changeover Expert) is captured.

If the machine's changeover for product A to product B was the changeover watched by the REC Team in Step 3 (Watch, List, Draw, and Brainstorm), then that same changeover for product A to product B must be tested. The new Downtime SOP developed during the REC Event is for a changeover from product A to product B.

1. Go to the production line where the machine is located.

   The entire REC Team goes to the plant floor, where the Test Team will perform the changeover using the new SOPs while the rest of the team observes.

2. Assemble around the machine.

   Changeover Experts: Go to the side of the machine and the position on the machine where you will perform the first task on your SOP.

   Coaches: Stand behind the Changeover Expert you're coaching.

   Spaghetti Makers: Stand behind the Coach where you can get a good view of the Changeover Expert for which you will create a Spaghetti Diagram.

   Timekeeper: Stand at the back of the machine.

   REC Coordinator: Stand wherever one or both of the Changeover Experts and the machine are visible. (The REC Coordinator will move around the machine during the test to observe both Changeover Experts.)

   REC Team Members: Stand at a short distance from the Test Team.

3. Test the ReducedEffort Downtime SOPs.

   During the Test session, Key members of the Test Team have the responsibilities described below.

   Responsibility: Timekeeper

   a. Jot down the start time of the changeover.

      Record only the start-up time of the changeover. Do not record the start-up times of the individual operators (Changeover Experts).

   b. Jot down the time the changeover was completed (when the Changeover Experts complete the Downtime SOPs).

   c. Calculate how long the machine was down to do the changeover (elapsed time, from start to finish).

   d. Record the total machine downtime with the new SOP.

Responsibility: Coaches

a. Follow the Changeover Expert and call out tasks, one by one, as the operator performs the changeover.

The challenge is to call out (or shout, in a noisy environment) the next task before the Changeover Expert has finished the current task.

EXAMPLE: While the Changeover Expert is

The Coach reading the tasks of the new Downtime SOP to the Changeover Expert, who has never done them in this sequence before

performing task 47, the Coach needs to call out task 48. The Changeover Expert should never have to turn around and ask the Coach, "What's next?"

b. Jot down on the SOP document brief reminders about things that need to be discussed during the Debrief session.

Responsibility: Changeover Experts

a. Complete each changeover task called out by your Coach.

b. Save any concerns and suggestions for the Debrief segment of the REC Event.

While the Changeover Expert is performing the changeover test, he may want to engage the Coach in a discussion about some task that is not in the correct sequence. Remind the Changeover Expert that the Coach will take notes as the changeover test is being performed and anything that needs to be changed will be discussed during the Debrief session. The Changeover Expert needs to follow the procedures without a discussion.

Responsibility: Spaghetti Makers

a. Follow the Changeover Expert, and each time he moves to another machine location or away from or back to the machine, draw a line tracing that movement on the Spaghetti Diagram.

b. Make a tally mark at the bottom of the drawing for each move the Changeover Expert makes.

Responsibility: REC Coordinator

a. Observe the changeover, and collect information to present at the debriefing and/or to management.

Make note of any issues, suggestions, or questions to discuss during the debriefing.

b. Take photos and/or short videos of important aspects of the new ReducedEffort changeover process.

4. Return to the conference room.

Spaghetti Maker, Changeover Expert, and Coach

The Coach following behind the Changeover Expert and reading the next task before the previous task is completed

The Spaghetti Maker (foreground) and the Coach (background) walking with the Changeover Expert as he moves about the machine doing his tasks

I'm often asked if we are going to video-record the entire changeover during the Test and Retest sessions, and I always answer no. Here's why: The Debrief occurs immediately after the first test while everything is still fresh in the Changeover Experts' minds. The improvements identified during the Debrief are implemented during the second test, which occurs immediately after the Debrief. Remember, Lean is all about eliminating waste. Filming these tests is wasted effort because no one is going to watch the entire changeover again. However, I do encourage you to take still photos and short video clips showing certain aspects of the new changeover process. These can be useful during the debriefing session and in explaining to upper management what was accomplished during the ReducedEffort Event.

8-D Evaluate the REC Downtime SOP test results.

This Debrief must occur immediately after the first test.

1. Call the rest of the REC Team back to the conference room.

   Responsibility: REC Coordinator

2. Discuss what worked and what didn't work during the Downtime SOP test.

   Responsibility: REC Coordinator with REC Team

3. Project the Downtime SOP documents on the screen so the REC Team can view the document.

   Responsibility: REC Coordinator

4. Discuss ways to improve the REC Downtime procedures.

   Responsibility: Test Team

5. Decide which improvements to the Downtime procedures to implement during the REC Event.

   Responsibility: Test Team

6. Revise the Downtime SOP to reflect improvements to be implemented during the REC Event.

   Responsibility: REC Coordinator

   a. Type any changes into the Downtime SOP document as directed by the REC Team.

   b. Print two copies of the revised Downtime SOP documents.

8-E Retest the new and improved REC Downtime standard operating procedures.

   Responsibility: Test Team

   The second test must occur immediately after the Debrief. It always amazes me how much effort and time are reduced by simply repeating the test, even when there are no changes to the Downtime SOPs.

   NOTE: If the test performed in 8-C.3 changed the machine from product A to product B, the machine will need to be changed back to product A prior to performing the Retest.

   1. Go to the production line where the machine is located.

      Make sure the changeover starts at the machine location indicated on the revised SOPs.

   2. Assemble around the machine.

      As in the first test, the Coach and Spaghetti Maker flank the Changeover Expert with whom they are partnered.

   3. Test the revised SOPs.

      During the Retest session, key members of the Test Team have the responsibilities described below.

      a. Record the changeover start time, finish time, and total machine downtime.

         Responsibility: Timekeeper

      b. Call out the tasks to the Changeover Expert, one at a time, in the sequence they appear on the revised SOP.

         Responsibility: Coaches

      c. Complete each changeover task called out by your Coach.

         Responsibility: Changeover Experts

d. Complete a Spaghetti Diagram of the Changeover Expert's movements during the changeover.

Responsibility: Spaghetti Makers

e. Observe the changeover, and collect information to present during the SOP finalization process.

Responsibility: REC Coordinator

4. Return to the conference room.

Upon completion of the Retest, all members of the REC Team return to the conference room where the REC Event is being conducted.

8-F Finalize the new REC Downtime standard operating procedures.

1. Call the REC Team back to the conference room.

Responsibility: REC Coordinator

2. Discuss the results of the second test of the modified Downtime SOPs.

Responsibility: REC Team

3. Review the before and after Spaghetti Diagrams.

Responsibility: REC Team

4. Discuss and decide whether any additional improvements should be made to the Downtime changeover procedure.

Responsibility: REC Team

5. Finalize the REC Downtime standard operating procedures.

Responsibility: REC Coordinator

a. Update the REC Downtime standard operating procedures, if and as necessary.

b. Generate the final Downtime SOP documents.

6. Congratulate everyone on a job well done.

Responsibility: REC Coordinator

This is an opportunity to praise your fellow workers. Lean is all about respect for people. Seize the opportunity to praise them for the work they have done. This is also an excellent time to bring in upper management, such as the VP of Manufacturing and/or VP of Engineering, so they can hear the results directly from the people who did the work. Having the opportunity to share a success story with upper management is not a common occurrence in a line operator's career.

The end result of a one-week ReducedEffort Changeover Event is a standard operating procedure that not only significantly reduces effort and time, but is also easier and more enjoyable for workers to do. No other documented process I am aware of addresses how to coordinate a person or a group of people to efficiently perform a series of tasks, such as in a machine changeover. Of course, the REC system is not limited to machine changeovers; it can be and has been applied to myriad procedures that require a series of tasks to complete.

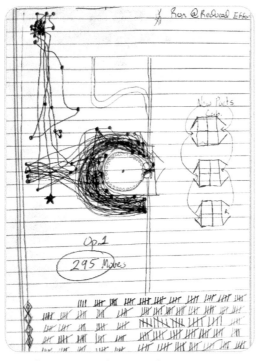

Before REC: The Spaghetti Diagram drawn while watching the changeover video shows 295 moves for CE1.

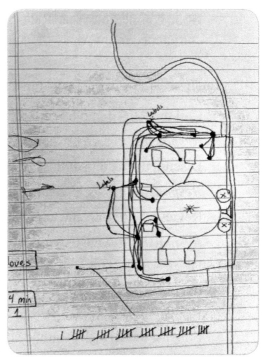

After REC: The Spaghetti Diagram drawn while watching the new REC Downtime SOP being tested shows 36 moves for CE1.

8 TOOLS

In one week, this REC Team reduced the changeover down-time by 58%.

While watching the video, whenever the Changeover Expert is seen picking up a tool, the Parking Lot Attendant or the REC Coordinator should ask if a quick-change device could be installed on the machine to eliminate the need for a tool. When you can eliminate the need for a tool, effort is reduced.

Consider the nonproductive time and effort that goes into using a tool. First, the Changeover Expert has to go get the tool, which involves walking to a tool box or a tool board. If the tool is not there, he or she has to remember where it was last used. Once the tool is found, the Changeover Expert walks back to the machine and uses the tool, which requires work. The Changeover Expert then needs to either place the tool down on the machine or return it to the tool box or tool board. When this tool is needed again, he or she needs to remember where they last put it. All of this is unnecessary work.

I don't think tools are needed to do changeovers. Yes, you heard me right. I believe quick-change devices can be used in place of nuts and bolts, eliminating most, if not all, tools. Tools should be reserved for machine maintenance and rarely, if ever, for changeovers.

During REC Events, I lay out about 50 pounds of quick-change parts that can be used to eliminate the need for tools. When a REC Team comes up with an idea on how one of these quick-change parts can be used to reduce their labor, the parts need to be ordered immediately and installed on the machine during the REC Event, prior to testing the new SOP.

This fast action accomplishes several things:

- It demonstrates how responsive the company is to employee ideas.
- You find out quickly if the part is going to work. If something is going to fail, then you want it to fail quickly so you can move on to what will work.
- It proves that the employees are empowered to make decisions and to try new ways to reduce their effort.
- It demonstrates that the company is willing to spend money on ideas from their employees.

A REC Team member studying how a quick-change part might be used to eliminate the need for a tool

- It prevents the idea from landing on a Parking Lot list that won't be accomplished for weeks following the REC Event.
- If the idea doesn't work, a discussion can begin with the REC Team, while they are all together, to come up with another idea that will work.

Something amazing occurs when people hold these quick-change parts, and it doesn't occur by just looking at pictures of them. People begin to imagine how the quick-change parts can be used. So, before you conduct a REC Event, I highly recommend that you order one of each of these parts so that you can pass them around for everyone in the event to hold while you explain how each of these devices might be used.

A list of quick-change devices can be found in Appendix II. You will notice that most of these are supplied by McMaster-Carr. The reason for this is that McMaster-Carr can deliver these parts overnight for next day delivery.

Tools are occasionally required, but sometimes they can be modified to reduce effort. Take, for example, the NASCAR race gun (air-impact wrench) that is used to remove lug nuts. The gun is never shut off as the wheel changer moves from one lug nut to the next; the socket is jammed onto each lug nut while the gun is running at 18,000 rpm. This is possible because the inner sharp faces of the socket are ground off so there is only enough flat surface to remove the lug nut. A spring is also installed in the socket to push the lug nut out of the socket before the socket lands on the next lug nut. This is an excellent example of Lean thinking. By making these modifications to the air-impact wrenches, all wasted effort is eliminated.

Race gun (air-impact wrench) removing lug nuts at 18,000 rpm

NASCAR race-gun socket with lug-nut removal spring

Following are photographs showing the elimination or modification of tools to reduce effort. Many of these quick-change devices are listed in Appendix II.

Before REC: This bearing (right) was moved during changeovers by screwing the all-thread in or out.

After REC: The all-thread was replaced with round stock that had three holes drilled in it for the three bearing positions. A pin on a lanyard was used to locate the correct position. (See Appendix II, item 7.)

When using a pin, I recommend always purchasing it with a lanyard. Then, effort is reduced because the Changeover Expert will always know where the pin is when it's time to insert it back into a hole.

Before REC: This Changeover Expert used a nozzle on a hose to clean the machine. But he found it difficult to see when the area was clean.

After REC: The light was attached to the spray nozzle with a clamp made in the company's shop.

After REC: A light was mounted on the spray nozzle, making his cleaning job much easier.

Before REC: A hand crank was used to adjust the conveyor width. This was a difficult job.

After REC: The socket was cut off the hand crank and welded to a shank that could be chucked in a cordless hand drill. The job is now easy.

Before REC: Bolts were used to hold these fixtures in place.

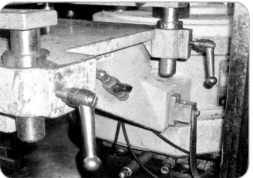

After REC: Adjustable handles replaced the bolts. (See Appendix II, item 4.)

After REC (left): A quick-install knob with a threaded-through hole replaced the nut. This nut is quick to install, position, and remove. These knobs have an angled hole that allows you to tilt the knob to slide it over the threads and then straighten it to grip the threads. (See Appendix II, item 3.)

Before REC: This nut required a wrench to tighten the clamp.

Before REC: A bolt held an adjustable arm.

After REC: A hand knob replaced the bolt. (See Appendix II, items 1 and 2.)

Before REC: Adjustable rail clamps with infinite positions. These should be used only as a proof-of-principle to determine where the rails should be located and should never be left on the line as a permanent way to adjust the rails.

After REC: Quick-adjust head with fixed positions. These push-button adjusters (knob) lock into pre-determined notches on the shaft. (See Appendix II, item 14.)

Before REC: During the REC Event, it was observed that the Changeover Expert was required to turn this handwheel with great effort and many revolutions.

After REC: The REC Team made this pinned disk so that it could be chucked into a cordless drill.

After REC: Changeover Expert using a cordless drill and pinned disk, which made turning the handwheel very easy and quick.

Before REC: During a previous SMED Event, a Kipp clamping lever replaced a bolt that secured the slider onto the shaft. The slider location varied and typically required additional adjustments (wasted effort). (See Appendix II, item 4.)

After REC: During the REC Event, the Kipp clamping lever was replaced with a ball-nose spring plunger, threaded into the bolt hole. This Ball-Nose Spring Plunger precisely located the slider by dropping into detents drilled into the flat portion of the shaft. The Ball-Nose Spring Plunger served as a way to easily move the slider from one precise location to another and to firmly hold it in place. (See Appendix II, item 10.)

Before REC: During the REC Event, it was observed that the Changeover Expert had difficulty loosening the Kipp clamping lever due to its location on the machine. (See Appendix II, items 26 and 27.)

After REC: An eccentric clamp replaced the lever. (See Appendix II, item 23.)

Before REC: The Changeover Expert needed to locate the correct size wrench to loosen the bolt holding this machine member in place.

After REC: The REC Team replaced the bolt with a ratchet arm with crank handle, which stays on the machine at all times. (See Appendix II, item 5.)

Before REC: The machine guard had to be removed for inspection.

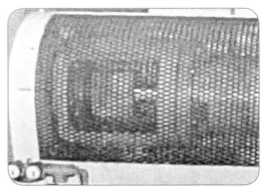

After REC: The REC Team painted the grate black to make the machinery behind the guard visible. Inspection can now occur during uptime instead of downtime.

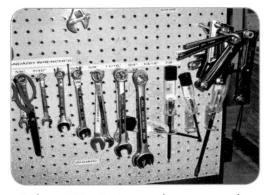

Before REC: During a changeover, the Changeover Expert would walk to the tool board to remove the needed tool.

After REC: The REC Team mounted a magnet on the machine guard to hold the needed tool, right at the point of use. If that same size wrench were required on the other side of the machine, another magnet to hold a duplicate wrench would be mounted there as well. (See Appendix II, items 26 and 27.)

THE REC PRESENTATION

What I'm about to describe is arguably the most important chapter of this book, alongside Chapter 7. The reason for this is because the REC Presentation can make a profound impact on hourly employees. At this point, the REC Team has devoted a week to reducing changeover downtime, and they have achieved amazing results. Now, as the last activity on the final day of the REC Event, the team will share that success with upper management.

The REC Presentation consists of a narrated slideshow (e.g., PowerPoint Presentation) that highlights the key components and results of the REC Event. Typically, a presentation like this would be made by the person leading the event, like the REC Coordinator. With the ReducedEffort process, the REC Team makes the presentation to management. The REC Coordinator prepares the slides and operates the projector, but he or she remains silent during the presentation while the individual team members discuss their respective slide(s). The exception to this is that the REC Coordinator may discuss the first and second slide.

Production workers in any plant have the potential to contribute brilliant ideas to reduce waste and increase company profits. The REC Presentation gives the people who work the line the rare opportunity to meet with upper management and talk about how they reduced the time it takes to do changeovers. This experience can help build a belief in themselves through the realization that their ideas are worth pursuing.

Additionally, it can be a turning point on the plant floor, where people start looking forward to coming to work. People who are valued enjoy their work more than those who feel ignored. People who feel valued and enjoy their work also tend to be more innovative, productive, and efficient.

It typically thrills the heart of a Lean leader or REC Coordinator to see their people rise up and speak boldly to a vice president, director, or even the president of the company. The REC Presentation cements the fact that the event made a lasting impact on their work lives. This impact shifts the paradigm to where people know that management respects their opinions and ideas, regardless of their position within the company. Remember, Lean is all about respect for people.

Management also typically responds very favorably to the REC Presentation, not only due to the results presented but also due to the engagement they see in their people during the presentation. I have had vice presidents and directors insist that they be invited to all REC Presentations within their company, and when they could not attend personally, they listened by way of a conference call.

This chapter lays the framework for the REC Presentation, providing a detailed description of how and when to prepare for and then make the presentation. This tried and true format not only will wow management and give the REC Team their much-deserved credit, it will also reduce the effort that goes into creating and conducting the presentation.

Preparing the REC Presentation

The REC Coordinator starts putting together the presentation on the first day of the REC Event and adds to it throughout the week. The presentation slides are created from digital photographs taken by the REC Coordinator and from documents created during the REC Event. The REC Coordinator creates the last slides and finalizes the slideshow on the last day of the event, while the REC Team is testing and retesting the new REC Standard Operating Procedure. This ensures that the presentation can be given on the last day of the event, while REC Team members are still excited about their success.

It is extremely important for the REC Coordinator to wait until after completion of Step 8 of the REC Event to reveal to the REC Team that they will be making the presentation. Many people fear making presentations, especially to upper management. So, if this information is not withheld until this point in the event, you may see many team members refuse to finish the event or call in sick the last day.

It is also important for all team members to participate in the presentation to demonstrate that the decisions made during the event were team decisions and not individual decisions. By having all team members describe the slides, it will be obvious to management that, during the event, every team member's input was encouraged and respected.

Invite Management to the REC Presentation

It is very important that management attends the presentation and hears what occurred during the event. The REC Coordinator is responsible for inviting upper management to the REC Presentation and encouraging their attendance.

The invitation to attend the REC Presentation can be sent to the plant manager, the directors of manufacturing and engineering, the VP of Engineering, members of the company's Lean initiative, those responsible for product quality, line supervisors, those responsible for training new hires, Changeover Experts on other shifts, and anyone else the REC Coordinator believes will benefit from the presentation.

The REC Coordinator can inform management that the REC process will be explained during the presentation, with particular emphasis on what was accomplished. There is no need to explain that the REC Team members will be making the presentation. Allow managers to be surprised and impressed when they hear, first-hand, the team members explain their results.

This invitation is typically sent during the first day of the event, and should specify the place, date, and time of the presentation. The presentation is scheduled for the afternoon of the event's last day. Therefore, if a one-week event is planned and the event begins on Monday, the presentation will typically occur on Friday, after lunch, in the conference room where the event occurred.

Additionally, the REC Coordinator can invite management to a catered lunch in the conference room prior to the presentation. Managers will appreciate the lunch, and it tends to relax everyone before the presentation. To confirm a commitment, the REC Coordinator can ask the invitee to RSVP.

Because it is difficult to predict exactly when the team will complete the event, the REC Coordinator should send additional emails to the invitees during the week to confirm the date, time, and location of the presentation.

Create the REC Presentation Slides

The REC Coordinator completes the following tasks on a daily basis throughout the REC Event.

1. Take photographs and/or videos of key components of that day's REC Event—i.e., team members, equipment, processes, tools, etc.
2. Select photos, videos, and documents ("images") created during that day's REC Event to include in the REC Presentation.
3. Convert each selected image into a presentation slide.
   - Download each photo, video, and document created that day into the digital slide presentation.
   - Label and number each slide. (Number sequentially from the first day through the last day of the event.)

NOTE: While the REC Team retests the new changeover procedures (Step 8 of REC Event, final segment), the REC Coordinator can return to the conference room and download the images from the Test and Debrief segments of Step 8 into the slide presentation.

4. Finalize the REC Presentation slides.

   The REC Coordinator performs these tasks after the REC Team has completed the Retest and returned to the conference room.

   • Update the slides, if/as needed, to reflect the final results.

     The retest will generally reduce the changeover time even more. When that is the case, the slide data will need to be updated to reflect the final reduced changeover time.

   • Snap the last photograph—of the REC Team holding the sign showing the changeover times before and after the REC Event.

For details on when and how to prepare and give a REC Presentation, please see the Sample REC Presentation section of this chapter.

I initially prepared the slides using PowerPoint on a PC but later switched to a Mac and generated the slides in Keynote, the Mac equivalent to PowerPoint. Additionally, I used Excel to generate the tables and graphs, but those can obviously be done in Numbers for Mac, instead.

Once the REC Coordinator has made the first set of presentation slides, he/she can simply modify those slides for future REC Events. Although the pictures and data will change with each event, the format will remain the same. This will reduce the effort in preparing for all subsequent REC Presentations.

Assign Presentation Slides to Team Members

The REC Presentation slides are divvied up among team members when the REC Team returns to the conference room after completing Step 8 of the REC Event (Test, Debrief, and Retest).

The slides are assigned to the REC Team in the following manner.

1. ***REC Coordinator:*** Inform the team that they will be doing the presentation to management and describe the process.

   • Explain that (a) each team member will describe one or more slides during the presentation, (b) you will show the slideshow now and ask for volunteers for each slide, and (c) if no one volunteers for a particular slide, you will assign that slide to someone who was involved in that activity.

- Explain that no one will have to stand in front of the room to make the presentation. As their respective slides come up on the screen, that team member will simply describe what is shown in the slide. This statement alone will reduce much of their concerns, and they will be more willing to participate, knowing they can remain seated at their tables. Some may also be relieved to learn that the lights will be dimmed (usually) so the slides will be more visible.

2. *REC Coordinator:* Show each slide to the team, one by one, and ask for volunteers to talk through each slide.

- If a person is pictured in the slide, that person usually volunteers or is asked to describe that slide.

- If no one volunteers for the slide being shown, pick a team member to discuss the slide. The REC Coordinator will need to assign some slides to certain people.

- Make sure no one is left out. Everyone must have at least one slide to discuss, and the slides should be divided up as equally as possible. The REC Presentation, like the REC Event, is a team effort.

3. Write down the slide number(s) assigned to each team member.

- *Presenter:* When a team member volunteers or agrees to talk about a particular slide, that team member writes (on a Post-It) the number of the slide he/she will be discussing.

- *REC Coordinator:* He or she may want to keep a master list of who is discussing each slide. There is little need for the presenters to write down what they are going to say or to practice what they will say. Each presenter should give a spontaneous, unscripted description of the slide.

4. *REC Coordinator:* As each slide is assigned, explain to the assigned presenter the "topic" of the slide, to give the person some ideas on what to say.

5. Run through the presentation slides to ensure that everyone knows which slide(s) they will be presenting to management.

- *REC Coordinator:* After all the slides have been assigned and the topics have been given to each presenter, quickly click through the presentation, one slide at a time, calling out each slide number.

- **Presenter:** The REC Team member assigned to talk about a slide responds "That's me" when the coordinator calls out his/her slide number. The presenter does not need to describe the slide until the actual presentation occurs. This quick run-through is just an opportunity for the presenters to see the slides again and a reminder to watch for the numbers of the slides as they come up during the presentation.

This preparation for the presentation typically requires no more than 30 minutes. Afterward, management will enter the room and take their seats. The REC Coordinator will welcome everyone to the REC Final Presentation and, if needed, ask each person in the conference room to give their name and job title. After these introductions, the REC Coordinator will show the first slide and the REC Presentation will commence.

Sample REC Presentation

This section features actual slides from a real-life REC Presentation and outlines a process you can use to prepare and give your REC Presentation.

Highwood USA of Tamaqua, Pennsylvania (www.highwood-usa.com/), has graciously consented to share their REC Presentation in this book. I especially want to thank Danielle Hess, who was plant manager during the REC Event and is now President and CEO, for allowing the inclusion of their slides in this chapter. Before I walk you through Highland's REC Presentation and the presentation process itself, let's take a closer look at the company and their REC experiences.

Highwood USA was founded in 2003 with the vision of "carefree backyard living." Their goal was to produce eco-friendly materials that mimic the look of nature's finest materials and that provide years and years of durability with minimal maintenance. They produce "nature's closest rival," a synthetic profile that is used in a variety of outdoor applications, including spa cabinets, playsets, pergolas, and their own line of Highwood Brand outdoor furniture.

The majority of REC Events I have conducted were performed on packaging lines in which there were fillers, cappers, case packers, etc. Highwood is different. They extrude synthetic lumber on their manufacturing lines. For this event, the REC process was applied to their extrusion line, not to their packaging line. The application of the REC process at Highwood is further proof that this process works on any plant floor where one or more people are performing a series of tasks.

Danielle Hess put together a REC Team whose members were innovative, highly skilled, and knew their jobs well. Like every company where the REC process is executed, they achieved amazing results within one week.

When Highwood-USA changes from one tool to another (one profile shape to another), they need to change the heavy extruding dies and the associated equipment. Prior to the REC Event, their changeover times often exceeded 5 hours, with the fastest being about 3 hours. During the REC Event, this changeover time was reduced to 45 minutes—a 75% reduction in time. Additionally, the number of tasks performed by the changeover expert prior to the REC Event was 2,567. During the REC Event, the number of tasks was reduced to 134 tasks.

What follows is the actual presentation the Highwood REC Team presented to management on the final day of the REC Event. I suggest assembling your slides as outlined below, at least for the first couple of REC Events you conduct. This will give you a good understanding of the reasoning and placement of the slides. This is just a suggestion and the way I did it. The presentation evolved over time and has a proven track record, but you may want to develop your own. What's most important is that a team-driven REC Presentation occurs on the last day of the event.

During the REC Presentation, you will move through the slides very quickly. The REC Presentation should take no more than 30 to 45 minutes, but plan on scheduling one hour to allow for questions and comments.

Below each Highwood slide, the following information is provided to assist the REC Coordinator in preparing the presentation:

- **Reference:** Where this slide is discussed in this book

- **Description:** What is depicted in the slide

- **When:** When each slide can be prepared during the REC Event. Adhering to this recommendation will dramatically reduce the REC Coordinator's work on the last day.

- **Purpose:** The reason management might be interested in this information

- **Who:** The person who should discuss the slide during the presentation. Remember, each REC Team member gets to talk about at least one slide. As a reminder, the following is a list of the roles for the people participating in a REC Event (Chapter 7, Step 3-A):
  - REC Coordinator
  - Changeover Expert
  - Coach
  - Spaghetti Maker

    – Parking Lot Attendant
    – Task Writers
    – Task Poster
- **Topic:** Suggestions about what the presenter can say while the slide is shown

Slide 1

Reference: N/A

Description: This is your introductory slide. Slide 1 features a photograph of the machine that is the focus of the changeover for the REC Event and a label specifying "ReducedEffort Changeover" as well as the name of the machine, the name of the company, the location, and the date. Import this picture into the presentation slide as the background, and then add the label (text) to the slide. If you prefer, you can fade the picture to make the text more visible. On the bottom left and/or bottom right, you can include a picture of the product that is produced on this machine. In this Highland slide, the product pictures show extruded lumber used for decks and rails.

When: Prepare this slide long before the last day of the event. You can snap the picture of the machine on the first day when you walk with the team to the production line in order to view the machine.

Purpose: To let managers, VPs, and others who have not been following the REC Event know to which machine the REC process was applied

Presenter: The REC Coordinator or a Lean manager/production manager who was involved in the REC Event

Topic: Explain why this machine was specifically chosen for the REC process.

Slide 2

Reference: Chapter 7, Step 3-A

Description: Slide 2 shows all the people who were on the REC Team for this event. During the event, snap a headshot of each person on the REC Team. After importing all the headshots, add the names of each individual under their respective photo. It is extremely important to spell their names correctly. You can usually get the correct spellings from an HR person, if you would rather not ask each team member.

When: Start preparing this slide after Day 1 of the event and well before the last day. Don't tell REC Team members that their pictures are going into a final presentation. You do not want them to know you are preparing a slideshow for management.

Purpose: To identify and give recognition to the people who participated in the REC Event. This is an opportunity to introduce management to the people who do the daily work on the line. Typically, very few people want their picture taken, especially this early in the event, but this is an important slide for the REC Presentation. They are going to accomplish something great during the REC Event that most managers think impossible. Acknowledgment will be due them.

Presenter: The same person who described Slide 1

Topic: Introduce each REC Team member.

Slide 3

Watch Video & Capture Tasks

Reference: Chapter 7, Step 3-B

Description: Slide 3 shows how the event started—with watching the changeover video that was made before the REC Event began. This slide features two images: a photo of the video screen and a photo of the group watching the video. Both photos are taken while the REC Team watches the video on Day 1 of the REC Event. After importing the images onto a slide, add a caption to briefly describe each image.

Note: As you can see from the various slides in the Highland REC Presentation, captions are used to help keep the viewer focused on what the slide is attempting to show.

When: These photographs are taken the first day of the event, and the slide can be made soon afterward.

Purpose: To explain how every task was captured by watching the video of the Changeover Expert performing the tasks

Presenter: The changeover expert who was videotaped is a good choice to discuss this slide.

Topic: The presenter can talk about being videotaped while they were work-ing and how they felt about that. The presenter can describe what a task is and how it was captured, in minute detail, on a Post-It.

Slide 4

Reference: Chapter 7, Step 3-B

Description: Slide 4 shows the number of tasks that were required to do the changeover prior to the REC Event. This is an impactful slide be-cause no one, not even the person doing the work, imagined how many tasks were required. The total number of tasks is the caption of this slide.

When: This photo is taken after all the Post-Its are on the wall, upon com-pletion of watching the video. In this Highland slide, the camera was held close to the wall to show the Post-Its from the first to the last of the tasks.

Purpose: To convey how difficult the changeover was and why it took so long to complete it. Upper management is generally shocked at the num-ber of tasks.

Presenter: The Task Writer or Task Poster typically discusses this slide.

Topic: This is an opportunity to explain how every task was captured as the video was watched. It might also be an opportunity to explain a typi-cal task and the number of Post-Its used to describe every detail of the task.

Slide 5

Capturing Ideas on Parking Lot

Reference: Chapter 7, Step 3-B

Description: Slide 5 shows all the ideas generated during the REC Event and written on the Parking Lot flip-chart pages.

When: This picture can be taken after completing Step 3 (Chapter 7). The photo can capture an image like the one on this Highland slide, or alternately, you could use a smartphone to take a photograph of the printed page of ideas and then download those digital images into the presentation.

Purpose: To show the number of ideas contributed by REC Team members and to emphasize the value of capturing every idea without debate

Presenter: The Parking Lot Attendant generally talks about this slide.

Topic: In the true sense of brainstorming, all ideas were written down without debate and without judgment. The total number of ideas can be stated, and the presenter can talk about some of the ideas that were implemented during the REC Event.

Slide 6

Priority Key	Impact on Effort Reduction	Feasibility
1	Little Impact	Difficult
3	Moderate	Moderate
5	High Impact	Very Easy

Parking Lot Ideas	Impact on effort reduction	Feasibility	Priority	Responsible Individual & Date
1. Idea A	1	1	1	Adam xx/xx
2. Idea B	3	5	15	Joe xx/xx
3. Idea C	5	5	25	Mary xx/xx
			0	
			n	

Prioritized Parking Lot Ideas

Reference: Chapter 7, Step 4

Description: Slide 6, which is discussed in Step 4 (Chapter 7), is generated in Excel or Numbers. (Highwood's ideas were purposely excluded from this slide).

When: A snapshot of a portion of the Prioritized Parking Lot Ideas is taken after completing Step 4 (Chapter 7). This snapshot can be a photograph of the first page of the Prioritized Parking Lot, taken with your smart phone or a screenshot captured from your computer. (With Mac, I used Grab.)

Purpose: To show the process used to prioritize the ideas that were captured in the Parking Lot. It is important for management to understand that there was a process for choosing why ideas were implemented, simulated, or held for future development. Additionally, this slide shows that individuals were assigned to implement the ideas by an agreed-upon date.

Presenter: The Parking Lot Attendant (the same person who discussed Slide 5) or any team member can discuss this slide.

Topic: The presenter may discuss how the ideas with the highest rating were either implemented or simulated during the REC Event. (Ideas were simulated if there was insufficient time during the week.) The presenter may discuss how one idea was simulated and that simulation is a way to demonstrate savings if the idea were implemented.

Note:　　　This is an excellent way to begin budgeting talks for an idea, while management is present.

Slide 7

Moving Downtime Tasks to Uptime Tasks

Reference:　Chapter 7, Step 5

Description: Slide 7 shows the first step in reducing the required tasks to be performed. In this photo, the REC Team is reading through all the tasks and deciding which tasks can be moved to uptime (performed while the machine is running) and which tasks are now trashed, based on ideas that will be implemented during the week (of the REC Event).

When:　　　This picture is taken while the team is reading each task and engaged in moving the task Post-Its to the Uptime and Trash walls.

Purpose:　To demonstrate and to help management understand how tasks were eliminated based on the prioritization of the ideas (Slide 6)

Presenter:　A Task Writer or Task Poster discusses this slide.

Topic:　　The presenter can discuss how this orderly process works.

Slide 8

Reference: Chapter 7, Step 5

Description: Slide 8 is a supportive slide to Slide 7 and shows the "bucket brigade" as described in Step 5-E (Chapter 7).

When: This picture is taken at the same time as Slide 7.

Purpose: To further management's understanding of the process of using a Post-It for every task and to show the orderly process for removing tasks that are no longer needed

Presenter: A Task Writer or Task Poster discusses this slide.

Topic: The presenter may talk about how writing down the tasks was difficult but they later understood the importance of capturing tasks in great detail.

Slide 9

Reference: Chapter 7, Step 5-E

Description: Slide 9 shows the tasks that are no longer needed.

When: This picture is taken after all the trashed tasks are on the wall or flip chart.

Purpose: To offer a visual image of what is possible when the workforce is empowered to make changes to the process. Management will be impressed with how many unessential tasks could be eliminated. Some teams place all of these "trash" Post-Its in a box and present it to a manager. Managers sometimes keep this box of Post-Its on their desk as a reminder of the unnecessary tasks that will never again be needed.

Presenter: A Task Writer or any team member

Topic: The number of tasks that are no longer needed can be stated. The Post-Its do not need to be counted to determine the number of trashed tasks. This number can be calculated using this equation:

Total number of Post-Its (Slide 4) – number of uptime tasks – number of downtime tasks = number of trashed tasks

Slide 10

Reference: Chapter 8 and Appendix II

Description: Slide 10 shows an assortment of quick-change parts.

When: This picture can be taken when the quick-change parts, which are shown during the REC Event, are laid out on a table. This assumes that devices in Chapter 8 and Appendix II have been purchased for "show and tell" during the REC Event. Once you have taken this photo, you can use the same photo and slide for any future REC Events.

Purpose: To show that the REC Team looked at quick-change parts that could be used to reduce changeover effort

Presenter: Any team member who installed a quick-change part on the machine or a mechanic who was on the REC Team

Topic: The presenter could explain that when quick-change parts are seen and held by members of the REC Team, ideas start flowing on how they can be used to replace nuts and bolts, with the goal of a tool-less changeover.

Slide 11

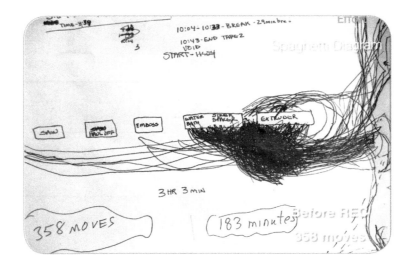

Reference: Chapter 7, Step 3-B

Description: Slide 11, the Spaghetti Diagram, shows the number of moves required to perform the changeover prior to the REC Event.

When: This picture can be taken at the conclusion of watching the changeover video, in Step 3 of the REC Event (Chapter 7).

Purpose: To dramatically illustrate how many times the Changeover Expert moved from one location to another, prior to the REC Event

Presenter: The Spaghetti Maker should discuss this slide.

Topic: The presenter can explain that these moves were captured as the REC Team watched the video of the changeover. The presenter can also explain how a move is defined, as specified at the beginning of Step 3 (Chapter 7). The number of moves and the changeover time, which are shown on the Spaghetti Diagram, are important numbers for management to know. This may also be an opportunity to discuss how a second Changeover Expert could dramatically reduce the effort of the changeover.

Slide 12

Reference: Chapter 5

Description: Slide 12 shows the REC Team gathering around the machine to discuss changes.

When: This picture can be taken any time the REC Team is discussing how the new changeover procedures will be executed or how a new quick-change part will be used.

Purpose: To show managers how the team became engaged with each other to make the best decisions. It can also convey the benefit of a work force that is empowered to make decisions without having to ask permission to make the changes.

Presenter: Any REC Team member

Topic: The presenter can describe what the team was discussing or talk about how everyone came together to make group decisions regarding the changes. The presenter may also discuss how the organization can profit from empowering its employees.

Slide 13

Reference: Chapter 8

Description: Slide 13 shows a modified clamp. In this Highland slide, the "Before REC" clamp was held together with three screws, each of which had to be removed before the clamp could be removed. The "After REC" part shows how the screws were replaced with a hinge, making removal of the clamp tool-less and much easier.

When: This picture is taken after changes are made. Pictures can be taken with the parts on or off the machine.

Purpose: To demonstrate to managers that the machine changes were made and the rules for making changes were followed. (See Step 2-E, Chapter 7.)

Presenter: Any REC Team member, but typically a mechanic or person who made the changes

Topic: The presenter describes each change made and the advantages of the change. An additional topic may be to describe how changes were only made if they could be reversed, in the event the modification didn't work.

Note: Only one Before REC and one After REC part is shown in this presentation. Typically, there will be several slides showing additional Before REC and After REC improvements.

Slide 14

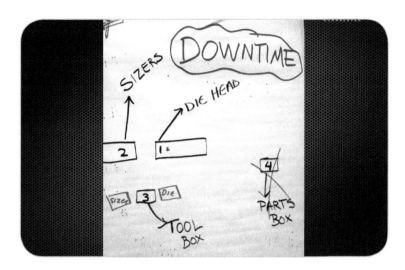

Reference: Chapter 7, Step 6-A

Description: Slide 14 is a photograph of the hand-drawn Choreograph Master Drawing, with numbered locations marked.

When: This image is taken any time after the drawing is made.

Purpose: To show the locations where the Changeover Expert needs to do work to perform the changeover

Presenter: Any REC Team member

Topic: The presenter may discuss how this Master Drawing was first used to identify where each task is performed and then used to make sure all tasks at one location were completed prior to moving to the next location.

Slide 15

Reference: Chapter 7, Steps 6-E thru 6-F

Description: Slide 15 shows the REC Team members standing in line, waiting to receive tasks (Post-Its) for each machine location on the Location wall. Option: Top left is a video showing this process, while the photograph (bottom) is a still photo. Making videos as part of the presentation can effectively illustrate the actions of the team members.

When: This picture (and video) is taken as team members are doing this work.

Purpose: To give management a brief summary of the Choreography process

Presenter: Any REC Team member

Topic: The presenter can discuss (briefly, without getting into much detail) how the Choreography process works.

Slide 16

Choreograph Tasks

Reference: Chapter 7, Steps 6-E thru 6-F

Description: Slide 16 shows a continuation of the Choreography process. The choreography steps are not shown, because to explain this process would exceed the time allowed for the presentation.

When: This photograph (or short video) is taken while the Choreography is taking place. Pictures of every step of the Choreography are not needed.

Purpose: To provide management with additional detail about how the Choreography was performed.

Presenter: Any REC Team member. It could be the same person who discussed Slide 15 or another person who has not talked about a slide.

Topic: The presenter can discuss, briefly, how the Choreography process works. Keep in mind that management does not need to know the details of this process. They mainly want to see that a process was followed and that everyone was engaged in the decision making.

Slide 17

Slide 18

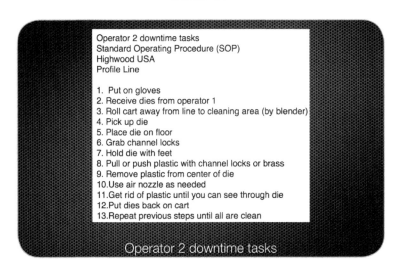

Slide 19

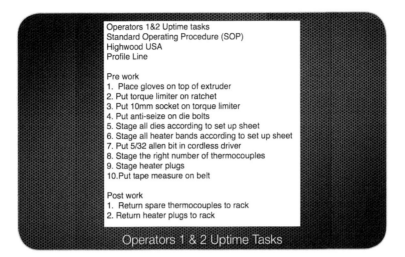

Operators 1&2 Uptime tasks
Standard Operating Procedure (SOP)
Highwood USA
Profile Line

Pre work
1. Place gloves on top of extruder
2. Put torque limiter on ratchet
3. Put 10mm socket on torque limiter
4. Put anti-seize on die bolts
5. Stage all dies according to set up sheet
6. Stage all heater bands according to set up sheet
7. Put 5/32 allen bit in cordless driver
8. Stage the right number of thermocouples
9. Stage heater plugs
10.Put tape measure on belt

Post work
1. Return spare thermocouples to rack
2. Return heater plugs to rack

Operators 1 & 2 Uptime Tasks

Reference: Chapter 7, Step 7-G

Description: Slides 17–19 show the Downtime Task and Uptime Task Lists for Changeover Experts 1 and 2 (Operators 1 and 2). As depicted in Slide 19, the Highwood team decided that the work of one Changeover Expert was now to be shared by two Changeover Experts. The Highland slides are screenshots of the task lists; the Grab application for Mac was used to do this. Alternatively, you could use a smartphone to take photographs of the first page of each printed task list and then download those digital images into the presentation.

When: The screenshots (or photos) of the task lists can be downloaded to the presentation application after Step 7 of the REC Event. Please refer to Figures 8, 9, and 10 in Step 7-G (Chapter 7).

Purpose: To show management sample pages of the new detailed Standard Operating Procedures (SOPs) for the changeover. The complete SOP does not need to be shown on the slides. Only the first page of each SOP is needed.

Presenter: Any REC Team member can discuss all three slides (17–19).

Topic: The presenter can describe how detailed the lists are and how these lists will serve to train others, with the goal of everyone doing it the same way.

Slide 20

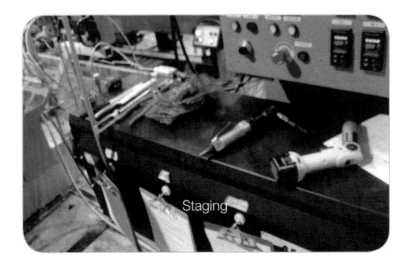

Reference: Chapter 7, Step 7-G, Figure 10. Staging is captured in the Uptime SOP. Staging can be seen in the last picture of Chapter 8, Tools.

Description: Slide 20 shows that tools and parts were staged at their point of use prior to testing (Chapter 7, Step 8).

When: This photo is taken the day of the test.

Purpose: To discuss the need to prep for the changeover while the line is still running

Presenter: Any REC Team member can discuss this.

Topic: The presenter can talk about how this staging was completed during uptime, prior to the changeover. The presenter might also discuss how important it is for parts to be repaired during uptime, so they are in good working order prior to the changeover. Another potential topic is how these tools/parts were or will be mounted to the machine at the point of use, instead of placing them in drawers or tool racks.

Slide 21

Slide 22

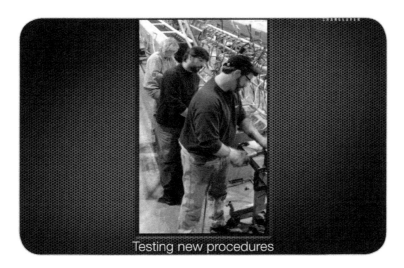

Slide 23

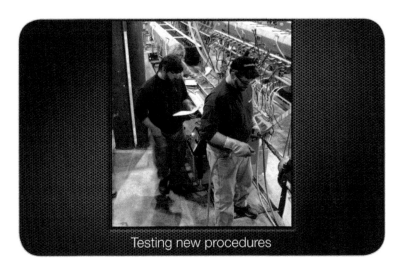

Testing new procedures

Slide 24

Testing new procedures

Slide 25

Testing new procedures

Slide 26

Testing new procedures

Slide 27

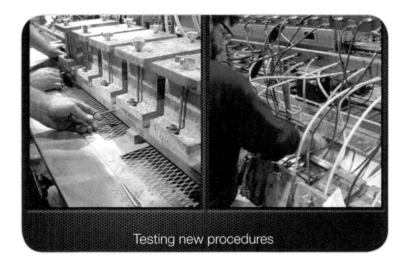

Testing new procedures

Slide 28

Testing new procedures

Reference: Chapter 7, Step 8

Description: Slides 21–28 show the testing of the new REC standard operating procedures (SOPs). These slides are a mixture of photographs and videos.

When: These photos and videos are taken during the new SOP test, prior to the Debrief and Retest segments of the REC Event.

Purpose: To show the Changeover Expert doing the work while the Coach reads each step and the Spaghetti Maker documents the moves. A video might also capture the Choreography of one or more Changeover Experts.

Presenter: The Changeover Experts are a good choice to discuss these slides. Other REC Team members can also join in with their observations. If any team members have not yet discussed a slide, this is an opportunity for them to share what they saw during the test and retest of the new SOPs.

Topic: The presenter can describe how the Coach read each step to the Changeover Expert because the expert has not yet memorized the sequence and can explain that, eventually, the expert will not need a Coach. Additionally, the presenter(s) may discuss how this same process can be used to train Changeover Experts on other shifts and new employees. The presenter may also note that the "best way" to do the changeover devised during the REC Event is the "one best way today," and that this one best way will continue to evolve as new ideas are tried.

Note: In Slide 26, Highwood's Changeover Expert is using a Sky Hook (see Appendix II, item 19) to lift the heavy dies. While watching the changeover video, it became obvious that unbolting and lifting each die was difficult, time-consuming, and a safety hazard. When the tools (See Chapter 8, Tools) were displayed during the REC Event, the team was shown pictures of the Sky Hook. The team immediately thought it could reduce their effort, so they ordered it and it was delivered overnight, with the condition that if it didn't work for their application, it could be returned. The empowered team didn't go through a time-consuming approval process to buy something that they assessed would reduce their effort. They received it quickly and tested it during the REC Event. The Sky Hook made it possible to lift all dies at once and was a key element in reducing their effort and time.

Slide 29

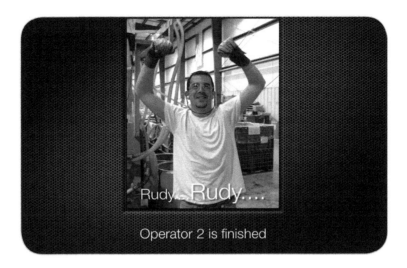

Reference: Chapter 7, Step 8

Description: Slide 29 shows the elation of a Changeover Expert as he finishes his tasks.

When: This unique photo was taken when the changeover tasks were completed. The Changeover Expert on your team may not do what Ben Beckett did here, but if you see an expert do something like this, it's worth capturing. When Ben finished his work in record time, he threw his arms up, and the REC Team chanted "Rudy, Rudy" from the movie of the same name.

Purpose: To show the elation of completing the work with ease and in record time

Presenter: Typically, the person captured in the photo (or video) presents this slide.

Topic: The presenter might discuss his or her work and how it felt to do it with less effort.

Slide 30

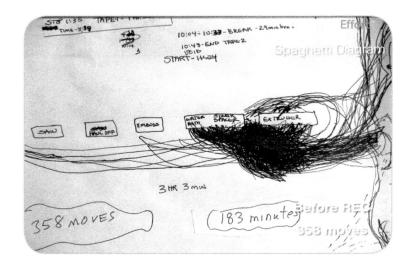

Slide 31

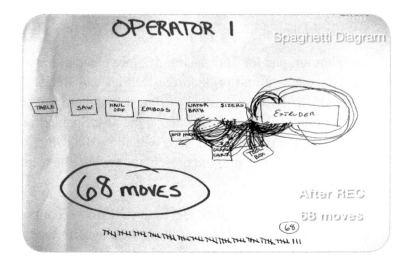

Slide 32

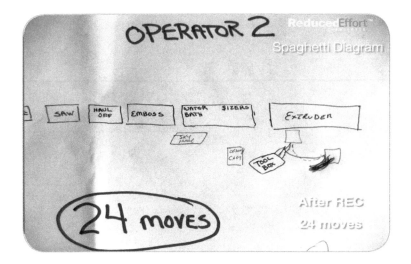

Reference: Chapter 7, Step 8

Description: Slides 30–32 are the "before" and "after" REC Spaghetti Diagrams. Slide 30 is a repeat of Slide 11, as a reminder of the "before" REC Spaghetti Diagram.

When: The photographs for Slides 31 and 32 are taken at the completion of the Test segment and prior to the Debrief and Retest (Step 8) segments of the REC process. The Retest Spaghetti Diagrams will be very similar to the Test Diagram, so the Test Spaghetti Diagram can be used for the presentation. This will allow the REC Coordinator to insert these pictures into the presentation while the team is conducting the Retest.

Purpose: To dramatically show that the ReducedEffort Changeover has reduced the moves required to perform the changeover. It can also give management an understanding of why, for example, two experts were needed to do the changeover instead of one.

Presenter: Ideally, the Spaghetti Maker(s) discusses Slides 30–32.

Topic: The presenter simply needs to read the number of moves before and after REC. The pictures tell the story.

Slide 33

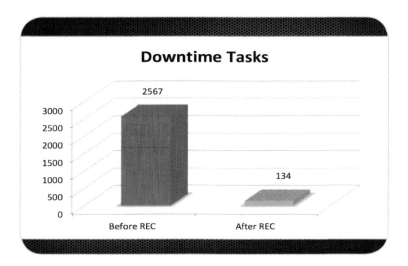

Slide 34

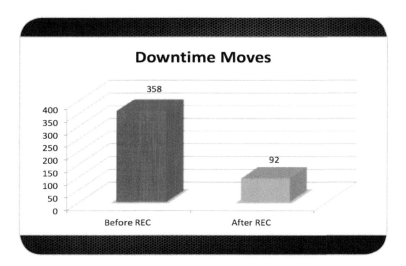

Slide 35

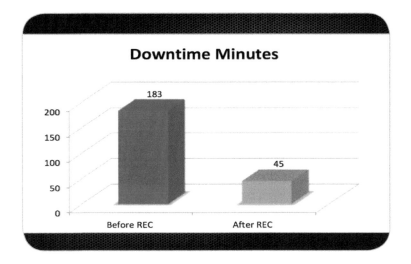

Figure 11

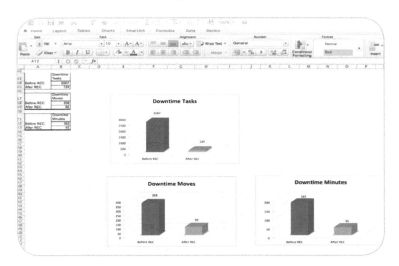

Reference: N/A

Description: Slides 33–35 are generated in an Excel spreadsheet and provide a graphic representation of the results.

When: The REC Coordinator generates the Excel spreadsheet prior to the REC Event. The downtime tasks and downtime moves can be put into the spreadsheet after completing Step 3-B (Chapter 7). The before and after times are placed in the spreadsheet after the REC Test.

Purpose: To give management an excellent visual comparison of the number of changeover tasks, moves, and minutes before and after the REC Event.

Presenter: Any REC Team member

Topic: The numbers on each slide can be read by the presenter.

Note: Figure 11 is a screenshot of the excel spreadsheet used to generate these graphs. Once this is set up for your first REC Event, producing the graphs for subsequent events is easy.

Slide 36

Changeover Downtime (minutes)	Changeover per week	Changeovers per month	Changeovers per year	Downtime per year (minutes)
183	6	24	288	52,704
Products	Lost opportunity	Increased production with 75% downtime reduction		
per minute	Products/year	Products/year		
3	158,112	118,584		

Reference: N/A

Description: Slide 36 shows how many more products per year can be produced by following the new REC standard operating procedures.

When: The REC Coordinator builds the Excel spreadsheet prior to the REC Event and completes the table after the REC Test.

Purpose: To demonstrate to management the need to sustain the work that the REC Team accomplished

Presenter: Any REC Team member

Topic: Emphasize the increased production as a result of the 75% downtime reduction.

Note: These numbers were generated in an Excel spreadsheet as follows:

1. Changeover downtime = the total minutes for the REC Changeover, captured while watching the video
2. Changeovers per week = This number is provided by the REC Team.
3. Changeover per month = changeovers/week x 4
4. Changeover per year = changeover/month x 12
5. Downtime per year = changeover downtime (minutes) x changeovers/year
6. Products per minute = This number is provided by the REC Team.
7. Lost opportunity = products/minute x downtime/year
8. Increased production with 75% downtime reduction = lost opportunity x 0.75

   Important: The 0.75 is specific to the Highwood event and derived from this equation:

   (Pre-REC changeover time – post-REC changeover time) / Pre-REC changeover time = % of time reduction

   (183 minutes – 45 minutes) / 183 minutes = 75%

Slide 37

Reference: N/A

Description: Slide 37 is a photo of the REC Team holding a sign showing the time reduction of the changeover. The percentage of reduction is shown in a caption below the slide.

When: Snap this picture after the team performs the Retest. Take large paper and marker to the production line, and make these signs immediately after the team finishes the second test (Retest) of the new changeover procedures. Gather the team in front of the machine, if possible, and have them hold the sign showing the time. Using Highwood's example, the percentage reduction in downtime is calculated as follows:

(Pre-REC changeover time – post-REC changeover time) / Pre-REC changeover time = % of time reduction

(183 minutes – 45 minutes)/183 minutes = 75%

Purpose: This is the most impactful slide of the entire presentation.

Presenter: No presenter is needed.

Topic: No description is needed. The slide speaks for itself.

This chapter has detailed how to prepare and give the REC Presentation. As previously stated, I suggest this format be followed at least once before modifying. The format may not work for everyone, but it does cover everything that most managers want and need to know after a REC Kaizen Event.

The REC Event begins the transformation of people believing that their ideas are valuable. This final presentation is an opportunity for management to engage with the people who actually did the work and to recognize them for reducing downtime. It is also an opportunity for managers to discuss with their people the impact that reduced changeover downtime has on the company's business and why it's important.

During the many REC Events I have conducted, I am always impressed by the innovative ideas that come from the people who work on the plant floor day after day. The REC Event simply offers them a process whereby their ideas can be tried, presented, and recognized.

Unfortunately, many people who work on production lines believe their ideas are not worthy of discussion. Time and time again, I have seen line workers who are experts at their jobs devalue their ideas and so keep their ideas to themselves.

Additionally, Changeover Experts, mechanics, and production technicians are typically an ignored group of people.

The reason brilliant ideas from these invaluable workers do not often come to the surface, except during a REC Event, is threefold:

1. Line workers are sometimes resistant to new ideas due to paradigm paralysis (as discussed in Chapter 2).

2. Employees on the plant floor lack the confidence to share their ideas due to their position in the company and/or their lack of formal education (as discussed in Chapter 5).

3. Managers sometimes discount ideas coming from those with lesser educational backgrounds (as discussed in Chapter 5).

Managers, engineers, supervisors, vice presidents, directors, plant managers, and presidents generally have more formal education than those who work on the plant floor. When a manager has spent a good portion of his or her life acquiring an education, he or she may find it easy to ignore or reject the ideas from someone with less credentials. *After all*, they seem to think, *how can someone who has barely graduated from high school possibly know more than those of us who have graduated from some of the finest universities in the country?*

If you don't believe this, find a person on the line who will give you an honest assessment and ask them if they feel their ideas are given as much weight as an idea from a manager. They will inevitably tell you that their comments are generally ignored and that management really doesn't want to hear their ideas. A great fault of managers is to discount someone's comments and opinions because they lack training and education.

Success doesn't depend on formal education. Nor does a person's value to the company that employs them and to the people with whom they work. A person's value should be based on his or her capabilities and contributions, not on their position or education. In the words of Thomas Edison, inventor of the incandescent light bulb, the phonograph, the motion picture camera: "I have friends in overalls whose friendship I would not swap for the favor of the kings of the world."

Conducting a REC Presentation can edify and honor the hard-working experts on the plant floor. When these experts are empowered to do the right thing, they come up with some amazing ideas that will reduce their work and increase company profits. The people on the plant floor are the greatest resource any company has, and the REC Presentation is an opportunity for management to recognize this.

10 HOW TO SUSTAIN A REDUCEDEFFORT PROCEDURE

In one week, this REC Team reduced the changeover down-time on a capper by 66%.

With the REC system, because the effort of the Changeover Experts is reduced and because they are involved in the entire process, they have ownership of the new SOP. They are motivated to continue using the new procedure because it makes their life easier by reducing their effort.

Management, then, needs to support the way the Changeover Experts have decided to do it. These are the people who know more about doing this changeover than anyone in the entire plant, so no one—and I mean *no one*—should have the authority to override the new SOP. It is management's job to support what the Changeover Experts have decided. It is also incumbent on management to make sure that the items on the Parking Lot list get done in a timely manner. This reinforces the commitment management has made to the ReducedEffort process and sends a clear message to the Changeover Experts that the company supports their ideas and is willing to spend money to give them what they need.

I have seen effective ways and ineffective ways in which to sustain the ReducedEffort process beyond the REC Event. In my experience, the only approach that has worked consistently is as follows.

- The Changeover Experts who attended the REC Event continue to perform the new SOP that was derived from the process. A coach stands behind them during the changeover, reading aloud the list of tasks until the changeover operators have it memorized.

- The Changeover Experts who attended the REC Event teach the new SOP to any Changeover Experts who could not attend the REC Event, by becoming their coaches. They stand behind them and call out the list of tasks until the experts who are new to the SOP have it memorized. This is repeated until all Changeover Experts on all shifts for that particular machine are using the new SOP.

- A changeover meeting is conducted every week or every other week, but no less than that. (One meeting per month typically does not work.) The meeting includes all the Changeover Experts who do the changeover of this machine on all shifts. (One option is to hold the meeting between shifts, when all the Changeover Experts can participate.) The team members that were involved in the REC Event participate in the changeover meetings. This includes people who do not work on the line but were involved in the REC Event. Team decisions carry much more intelligence than individual decisions. So invite the whole REC Team, and do your best to get them there.

- During each changeover meeting, the REC Coordinator asks the operators what is working and what is not working. The SOP is then revised to reflect their comments.

- The Changeover Experts test the revised SOP on one machine changeover. If the changes don't work, then revert the SOP back to the way it was. If the changes work, continue to use this revised SOP. In either case, report the results at the next changeover meeting.

- The Changeover Experts record the changeover downtime for the revised SOP. This information is brought to the changeover meeting, where it is shared with the team. The team then discusses the results of the most recent changes to the SOP.

- The REC Coordinator continues to monitor the delivery of the items on the Parking Lot list by communicating with the responsible individuals specified on the list. This could mean coordinating the procurement of parts and/or tools, fabricating parts, modifying the machine, etc. Whatever is on the Parking Lot list that the REC Team said needed to be done must be done—ASAP.

- The REC Coordinator reports the status of the Parking Lot items during the changeover meeting.

- During these REC Team meetings, the members should be encouraged to continue reducing effort and time. As they continue to challenge their paradigms, innovative ideas will come to the surface. When these ideas are tested, additional ideas will be generated and tasks will continue to drop off the SOP.

Lean is all about respect for people and continuous improvement. The best way to perform a changeover was found during the REC Event. This new SOP is the best way today. Tomorrow, the team could build on what was done and find a better way. As has often been said: Lean is a journey, not a destination.

Never view your current position as having arrived. What is the "best way" today may not be the "best way" tomorrow. No matter how fantastic the results were from the ReducedEffort process, more can be done to lessen the effort and to drive down the time even further. Continue to encourage empowerment on the plant floor by letting your people try new things. Empowered people are generally happier people, and happier people are more apt to come up with innovative ways to reduce their effort to make their lives easier.

11 HOW TO INCREASE INNOVATION ON THE PLANT FLOOR

In one week, this REC Team reduced the changeover downtime on a filler by 68%.

An important element of establishing Lean on the plant floor is to respect everyone's ideas. To illustrate this, I'd like to tell a story about grocery stores in the late 1800s and early 1900s. At that time in America, a grocery store consisted of a counter with shelves behind it, where the merchandise was stacked to the ceiling. The customer would tell the clerk behind the counter what he wanted, and the clerk would climb up the ladder and retrieve the items from the shelves. The clerk would then total the charges for the items and bag the merchandise. The customer didn't even touch the merchandise until he or she got home and removed it from the bag.

There once was a young man named Clarence Saunders, who worked in one of these grocery stores. It was his job to stock the shelves and perform custodial duties.

Typical grocery store in early 20th Century America

One day on his lunch break, Clarence decided to visit the new restaurant that had recently opened down the street. He walked in and was amazed at what he saw. There were no waitresses or waiters taking orders at the tables. Instead, there was a stack of trays at the door and a long counter on which all the food choices were displayed. It was a new cafeteria-style restaurant. He picked up a tray, walked down the counter, and picked the food he wanted. At the end of the counter was the cash register, where he paid for his lunch.

After lunch Clarence ran back to the grocery store to tell his boss about what he had seen and about his new idea for a grocery store. He was very excited about this new idea and expected that his boss would be just as excited. As he started to share his idea, his boss interrupted him.

The first Piggly Wiggly grocery store

"I'm tired of all your crazy ideas, Clarence. You're fired!"

That didn't stop Clarence Saunders from thinking about and developing his idea, and he was successful in securing financial backing. On September 6, 1916, he opened the first Piggly Wiggly® grocery store at 79 Jefferson Street in Memphis, Tennessee.

As customers walked into Clarence's grocery store, they didn't present a list to the clerk behind the counter. They pushed a shopping cart, which Clarence invented, down the aisles, filling their cart with groceries they picked off the shelves and out of the cold storage cabinets, which he had also invented.

Piggly Wiggly, America's first self-serve grocery store chain

Clarence Saunders had invented the modern-day grocery store. This innovative man saw the waste associated with the proprietor-controlled grocery store and came up with an unheard-of solution that revolutionized the entire grocery industry: He developed a way for shoppers to serve themselves. His idea was wildly successful and forever changed the way people shop.

Piggly Wiggly today

Inside a modern Piggly Wiggly

He shifted the paradigm and caused all those stuck in the old paradigm to either change or go out of business. Clarence Saunders' former boss later said that he believed he lost a million dollars for every word he used to fire Clarence that day.

By 1932, the Piggly Wiggly chain had grown to 2,660 stores doing over $180 million annually. Piggly Wiggly was the first retail store to provide shopping carts, prices marked on every item, checkout stands, employee uniforms, refrigerated cases, high-volume and low-profit margin retailing, and a full line of nationally advertised brands. Everything you've experienced at Walmart was started by Clarence Saunders.

The same thing that caused Clarence Saunders' boss to miss the greatest opportunity of his life is, right now, stopping innovative ideas in corporations all across America. That killer of innovation is the way in which most people, including a company's upper management, respond when approached with a new idea. I have surveyed employees in many of the country's greatest companies. When I ask employees what kind of responses they receive when they present a new idea to someone in their organization, I receive the same basic answers, as follows.

"It won't work."

"It costs too much."

"We've tried that before."

"That's not your job."

"That's a lousy idea."

"No!"

"We can't interrupt production to try your idea."

"I'm not interested."

"That's not what you were hired to do."

"Get back to work."

"Who do you think you are, the president of the company?"

"Don't you have enough to do?"

"I'll think about it and get back to you."

I am confident that these responses will come as no surprise to you. I am also confident that if you are an innovator, you have heard many of these statements. These responses will kill a new idea before it is ever tried. What might be even worse than killing the idea is that it may kill the innovator. I don't mean that literally, but when you stop an innovator from sharing his ideas, you figuratively destroy him. If an innovator hears these responses often enough, eventually he will stop presenting new ideas to management.

Why are these naysaying statements the common responses to new ideas? Because new ideas represent change, and nobody wants to change. Change means work, and nobody wants more work. It is natural to reject new ideas, and most people do this automatically. Rejecting ideas takes zero effort, and it occurs every second of every day in every small business and in every large corporation in the world. New ideas cut across the established paradigm, and sticking with the existing paradigm is less work. Ideas are killed every minute of every day in manufacturing plants all across America. Bosses, managers, leaders, and executives at every level of every company need to be open to paradigm shifts.

There is a way to respond to the innovator that will not defeat the idea or the idea maker. When presented with an innovative idea, a more effective way to respond is as follows:

1. Make a positive statement about the idea.
2. State a benefit for the company if the idea works.
3. Ask, "How can you test your idea to prove that it works?"
4. Ask, "Is it reversible? In other words, can it be implemented and then a test performed without permanently altering existing equipment or current methods?"

The order of these steps is as important as the statements. When you make the first two statements, it tells the innovator that he is not being ignored and that you welcome innovative thinking. It also encourages the person to continue thinking innovatively and ensures that the innovator will tell you his future ideas. So, even if it seems like the most idiotic idea you have ever heard, it is important to always make those first two statements.

The third step addresses your concerns or what you suspect might be wrong with the idea. If you think that one part of the idea is flawed, then you would ask how that element could be tested. The fourth step assures that the innovator understands that if the idea does not work, he can put things back to the way they were before the idea was tried.

When you respond to an idea in these ways, the innovator will leave the discussion feeling encouraged, knowing that his innovative thinking is appreciated and that his idea was not rejected. He will also leave the discussion with the challenge of proving the idea and the confidence that if it doesn't work, there will be no disciplinary action because he will put everything back to where it was before the trial.

Many times, innovators don't know what to do with their ideas, so they approach their managers in an attempt to hand it off to someone who can implement it. Often, the manager sees this as their subordinate's attempt to pass the implementation work onto him. Many managers will reject ideas simply to prevent the dumping of work. Everyone already has more than they can do. However, when the manager asks, "How can you test the idea to prove that it works?" he has given the task of proving the validity of the idea back to the innovator. The manager has avoided this "dumping" and placed the responsibility of proof back on the innovator, where it belongs.

If the idea does not work, the manager usually will not hear about the idea again. The important thing here is not whether the idea was any good; what's important is that the innovator will come back to that manager with his next idea. That next idea may also prove to be of no value; even the tenth idea may have no merit. However, if the manager uses this approach, then he will hear the innovator's eleventh idea, which may be the paradigm shift that changes the course of the company. If the manager had responded to the first or fifth or tenth idea with "That's a lousy idea," he never would have heard that game-changing eleventh idea.

This way of responding to new ideas should be used every time someone approaches you with an idea. It is a simple way to overcome your own paradigm paralysis. When it is applied, innovation will be encouraged because it demonstrates great respect for people.

If you want to build a Lean environment in which people are continually improving the processes, you must establish an environment in which people are continually shown respect.

The Dupont Race team applies this principle during their morning meetings by stating that everyone's opinion is expected and everyone's opinion is respected. That deserves repeating. Everyone's opinion is expected, and everyone's opinion is respected. Think about that profound statement—which is far too uncommon in U.S. manufacturing plants.

Speaking of which, if you thought the Saunders' model for grocery stores couldn't be improved, think again. While on the Japan Study Mission in Japan, I visited a grocery store and saw how the Japanese have removed more waste from the process. They have multiples of three checkout stations, where your purchases are: 1) scanned, 2) paid for, and 3) bagged. At the first station, the checker has an empty cart on one side of the station, and you push your cart to the other side of the station. The checker scans the items from your cart and places them in the empty cart. You then push the cart of scanned items to an open pay station. After paying, you move your cart to an open bagging station, where you remove your items from the cart and place them in the bags. You don't need to wait in line because there are multiples of each of these stations where the scanning, paying, and bagging occurs. In addition, each station has an Andon light, so you can see at a glance where there is no waiting.

Contemporary Japanese grocery store

Lean is all about respect for people, and waiting in long checkout lines is not respecting people's time. In January 2018, the first Amazon Go grocery store opened in Seattle, Washington, featuring Amazon's proprietary "just walk out technology." Customers download the Amazon Go app to their smartphones, and as they enter the store, a turnstile scans the app to identify each shopper. Cameras and shelf sensors throughout the store record each item a customer picks up and places in a bag. After the customer has finished selecting and bagging everything he or she wants to purchase, he or she simply walks out of the store with the scanned merchandise and without stopping to pay. The customer's Amazon account is automatically charged for those "purchases" as soon as they exit the store.

The Japanese grocery stores and the Amazon Go store show great respect for customers' time by setting up a process that moves them quickly through the store. This is Lean at its finest. It is innovation at its finest.

Establishing a Lean environment in your operation requires innovative thinking from everyone. Encourage it. Don't kill it.

AFTERWORD

If we would only do the things we are capable of doing, we would literally astound ourselves.

—Thomas Alva Edison

In one week, this REC Team reduced the changeover downtime on a bag bundler by 87%.

After graduating from mechanical engineering school, I was hired by my dad to work at his company, Epoxy Coatings Company. As a young child I had watched him build his business from our home garage to a profitable business making and selling coatings to the fishing rod industry. He was a chemical engineer and wanted me to be the same, but due to my interest in cars, I became a mechanical engineer. After receiving my degree from California State University at San Jose, I was ready to start designing machines, but my dad needed a chemical engineer, not a mechanical engineer. He told me that chemists had tried for years to make a coating to replace the "fingernail polish" that fishing rod manufacturers then used to hold the threads, which in turn held the guides on the rods.

Guides held onto fishing rods with thread and then coated

This coating needed to be clear in color, dry fast, always remain flexible, and cure without any bubbles. No one had ever solved this problem, and he said that if I came to work for him and developed this coating, he would pay me a salary and give me 10% of the profit from the coating. That's all I needed to hear. That day I became a chemical engineer, and for the next two years I worked in a lab experimenting with one formula after another. I filled two lab books with one failure after another, but because of what he had always taught me, I kept accurate records of what I mixed together and documented my observations of the results. It was a rough two years. It's difficult to fail day after day. I was not a chemist, and I didn't know what I was doing, but I kept experimenting.

One day I noticed that the coating was clear, cured quickly, was flexible, and cured without entrapped bubbles. Wow, I'd done it! Or so I thought. I tried it again, but when I came back the next day, it had a milky film on the surface. I mixed a new batch, came back the next day, and it looked great. One day it would look great and I would mix a new batch of the same formula, and then the next day the new batch would have the milky film. Was the formula varying? Was I mixing it the same way and in the same order? Everything I was doing was the same, so what was causing this milky film?

Then I noticed that on the days the milky film appeared it was raining. I thought maybe the increase in humidity was causing it. So I put an infrared light over the coating while it was curing, and to my surprise, that solved the problem. The infrared light dried the surrounding air, which prevented the moisture in the air from adhering to the surface of the coating and causing the milky film. Now, I had the right formula and the right process.

Next, I developed a machine that could be used by manufacturers to apply this coating. The machine held 31 spinning rods and advanced the coating to a curing area, where infrared heaters removed all moisture. Working as a "chemical engineer" had enabled me to apply my mechanical-engineering training to design and build the machine.

We called the coating Thread Wrap Coating. Epoxy Coatings Company began selling the coating and the machine to Garcia, Fenwick, Daiwa, Shakespeare, and every other fishing rod manufacturer, and I made 10% of the profit on all the coatings we sold. In essence, I made money on every fishing rod sold in America for the next 10 years.

The reason I'm sharing this story is not to elevate myself but to make a point. I didn't know enough to know that it couldn't be done. I wasn't a chemist, so I had no boundaries, no preconceived ideas about what would work and what wouldn't work. The only thing I knew was to keep good records. Every day I would come to work and look at what I had mixed together the previous day and study the results. I learned what caused bubbles, what made the coating hard, what made it flexible, what kept it clear, and so on. This is known as *intelligent failure*. I learned from the failures and just kept trying. An important take-away here is that failure should be welcomed, not avoided. My dad understood this. He could have said that his son didn't know what he was doing and that I was wasting his money, but he didn't. Imagine, two years of failures! He just let me continue until I finally ran out of things that didn't work.

When you empower your workforce to make changes that directly make their jobs easier, people will try things that may not work. Let them continue trying until they succeed, and you will be amazed at the innovation that starts occurring on the plant floor. Lean is fun because people are free to innovate to make their jobs easier. Innovation can make the workplace an exciting place to be every day. People look forward to coming to work when they are allowed to make process improvements in areas that directly affect their work.

Thomas Edison, the most prolific inventor in history, had much to say about innovation, including: "If we would only do the things we are capable of doing, we would literally astound ourselves." "No experiments are useless." "Remember, nothing that's good works by itself, just to please you. You have to make the damn thing work." And "There are no rules here—we're trying to accomplish something."

Some of the most successful people in the world and throughout history have attested to the value of perseverance in the face of failure.

Dr. Albert Einstein said, "Anyone who has never made a mistake has never tried anything new."

Michael Jordan, one of the greatest basketball players of all time, said, "I have missed more than nine-thousand shots in my career. I've lost almost three-hundred games. Twenty-six times I've been trusted to take the game winning shot, and missed. I have failed over and over and over again in my life, and that is why I succeed."

Babe Ruth, the first baseball player to hit 60 home runs in one season said, "Never let your fear of striking out get in your way."

Wayne Gretzky, one of the greatest hockey players of all time, said, "You miss one-hundred percent of the shots you don't take."

Erin Brockovich, an unemployed single mother with no legal education who became a legal assistant whose research was instrumental in winning the largest toxic-tort injury settlement in United States history, said, "By learning from your mistakes, you will discover that they are not mistakes after all. They are learning tools. Do not be afraid to fail. Failure is the best route to finding success."

Thomas J. Watson, founder of IBM, said, "You're thinking of failure as the enemy of success. But it isn't at all. . . . You can be discouraged by failure—or you can learn from it. So go ahead and make mistakes. Make all you can. Because, re-member, that's where you'll find success."

In developing the Thread Wrap Coating, I experienced the power of these statements. Not being a chemist and being tasked to develop an innovative coating was like facing an insurmountable mountain. However, I knew in my heart I could find the right combination of ingredients and conquer every obstacle I encountered. It took two years, but it changed the course of my dad's company and had a lasting impact on my life.

I'm reminded of a great Biblical truth regarding believing:

> "And Jesus answering saith unto them, Have faith in God. For verily I say unto you, That whosoever shall say unto this mountain, Be thou removed, and be thou cast into the sea; and shall not doubt in his heart, but shall believe that those things which he saith shall come to pass; he shall have whatsoever he saith. Therefore I say unto you, What things soever ye de-sire, when ye pray, believe that ye receive them, and ye shall have them."
> —Mark 11: 22–24 (KJV)

Let your people try things that you may think will never work. Failure leads to success. In fact, you often can't have success without it, and you frequently can't successfully implement Lean manufacturing without it.

Charles Kettering, an American inventor, engineer, and businessman, said, "The biggest job we have is to teach a newly hired employee how to fail intelli-gently. We have to train him to experiment over and over and to keep on trying and failing until he learns what will work."

Paul A. Akers, CEO of FastCap and author of *2 Second Lean*, said, "I don't hire people to make parts; I hire them to improve the process of making parts." Paul's employees are required every day to come up with a new way to cut two seconds out of the process. In essence, he is telling them to change their process to make their work easier, and the metric he is using to determine the improvement is time. Reduce the effort, and time automatically decreases.

As your employees try new things, they will discover that some of their ideas do not work. That's okay. Through their failures, they will come up with other ideas that do work. Many people think of this as failure, but it is exactly the opposite. It is the foundation of success.

Keep in mind that the goal is to reduce effort to make jobs easier. As your people make their work easier, they will be motivated to continuously make more process improvements. As they continuously improve the process, they will eliminate waste everywhere and every day, which is what Lean is all about.

ReducedEffort® is a dynamic continuous-improvement process that yields consistent and sustainable results. It is the Lean way to quickly reduce the effort of any process involving a series of tasks that need to be done repeatedly. Remember, reducing the time is not the goal; reducing time is the result of reducing effort. Whenever effort is reduced, time will be reduced and safety will be increased, as well. It's not about rushing to complete the work faster. It's about systematically performing a predetermined set of tasks (procedure) that has been intelligently and efficiently planned. ReducedEffort is a proven method to eliminate wasted effort in order to increase productivity throughout the plant.

The ReducedEffort Changeover system sets a new standard for rapid changeovers. I have conducted hundreds of these events, and Changeover Experts are always thrilled with the results they achieved in just five days. I have had CEOs tell me that it is the first time they have seen some of their employees smile. Everyone wants to work less and make the same or more money. In any U.S. manufacturing plant, the Changeover Experts are typically an unappreciated group of people who are living, as Henry David Thoreau said, "in quiet desperation." The ReducedEffort Changeover system changes that.

ReducedEffort makes work simpler. There are no charts to keep, no graphs to post, and no time calculations to crunch. The REC method just focuses on reducing the effort expended by people doing their work. Once your people get the idea that it's all about making their jobs easier and their lives better, you will be well on your way to becoming Lean.

"That's awesome!" an operator at a major food manufacturer said after obtaining a 50% reduction in downtime with the ReducedEffort Changeover process. In four days, the operator's team had reduced a 44-minute changeover to 22 minutes.

His manager agreed. "The operators and maintenance workers . . . would have argued for weeks about how it should be done and never have come to a consensus. The ReducedEffort Event provides an interesting way of engaging all participants in coming up with time and effort reductions. Standard work is being sustained, and the principle works."

Brad Miller gives two thumbs up after he and his REC Team reduced the effort required to change over a labeler. This reduction of effort reduced the changeover downtime from 1 hour and 58 minutes to 24 minutes. That's an 80% reduction in downtime, and it was accomplished in one week!

This event has completely exceeded all prior expectations. This was unlike any process improvement I have ever been a part of. I really don't know if I can put a value on this training because this event will change my life for the next fifty to sixty years. This process could be applied to any and all aspects of work and life. I am very glad I was able to attend this class. Ron has taught me more than I could say. . . . Wow, what an eye-opening week!

—*Brad Miller, Process Improvement Coordinator, major beverage bottler*

APPENDIX I
THE EASY WAY TO CALCULATE
THE COST OF DOWNTIME

Calculating the true cost of downtime is difficult because it requires knowing all the direct and indirect costs, such as labor, power, etc. The equation, below, makes it simple by focusing on lost opportunity.

LO = 48 (a) (b) (c)

COD = (LO) (d)

KEY

Assumes 48 production weeks per year.

LO = Lost Opportunity (number of products not produced per year due to downtime)

COD = Cost of Downtime (USD per year)

a = Changeover downtime (minutes)

b = Number of changeovers per week

c = Products produced per minute

d = Revenue per product

EXAMPLE

LO = (48 wks/yr) (300 min/changeover) (4 changeovers/wk) (1980 products/min) = 114,048,000 products per year not produced due to downtime

COD = (114,048,000 products/year) ($0.02 /product) = $2,280,960 per year lost due to downtime

If the changeover were reduced by 30%, an additional 34,214,400 products (114,048,000 x .30) would be produced for an additional revenue of $684,288 per year (34,214,400 x $0.02).

APPENDIX II
NO TOOLS NEEDED

	Quick Change Device	Supplier	Part Number
1	Polished finish aluminum four arm knob	www.mcmaster.com	60965K31
2	303 stainless steel four-arm knob	www.mcmaster.com	4384K2
3	Quick-install knob with threaded-through hole	www.mcmaster.com	6032K11
4	303 stainless steel adjustable handle	www.mcmaster.com	6522K34
5	Ratchet arm with crank handle	www.lowellcorp.com; 800–456–9355	
6	D1 Dzus dart quarter-turn fasteners	www.southco.com	
7	T-handle push-button quick-release pin with lanyard	www.mcmaster.com	93750A190
8	L-handle push-button quick-release pin	www.mcmaster.com	90302A041
9	High profile push-button quick release pin with lanyard	www.mcmaster.com	94748A202
10	Ball-nose spring plunger with SS ball steel body and catch for ball-nose spring plunger	www.mcmaster.com	3408A65, 33545A21
11	Pull-ring retractable spring plunger; T-handle retractable spring plunger; L-handle retractable spring plunger; Twist-to-lock knob-style retractable spring plunger	www.mcmaster.com	8691A31, 31265A56, 8691A19, 8691A29
12	Candy timing and phasing hubs	www.candycontrols.com	
13	QuikLoc all steel shaft collars	www.quikloc.com/shaft.htm	
14	SystemPlast quick-adjust head (Suppliers rarely have these in stock, but they can order them.)	www.motionindustries.com, www.kamandirect.com	33298

	Quick Change Device	Supplier	Part Number
15	Septimatech unison modular rail system and quick changeover stars & guides	www.septimatech.com	
16	ASTRRA rail system	www.asthomas.com; 781–329–9200	
17	Roh-Lix linear actuators	www.zero-max.com; 800–533–1731	
18	Economy magnetic base	www.mcmaster.com	1878A22
19	Sky Hook	www.skyhook.cc; 800–475–9466	8560 (Sky Hook with cherry-picker base)
20	Quick disconnect couplings & hose fittings, 316 SS, food grade	www.banjocorp.com; 765–362–7367	
21	De-Sta-Co clamps	www.destaco.com; 1–888–337–8226	
22	Quick TeeJet diaphragm nozzle for wet booms to make inexpensive CIP systems	www.teejet.com	QJ17560A
23	Corrosion-resistant clamping handles with threaded stud (eccentric clamping handle)	www.mcmaster.com	5720K51
24	Metal lift-off surface-mount hinge	www.mcmaster.com	1151A82
25	Pull-release quick-disconnect surface-mount hinge	www.mcmaster.com	1305A54
26	Stainless steel magnetic tool holder	www.mcmaster.com	12325A36
27	Nickel-plated steel magnetic tool holder (stronger holding power than 12325A36)	www.mcmaster.com	6613A61
28	Quick-change cylinder locks to replace nuts & bolts	www.toolingtech-group.com/quick-change.asp	
29	Multiple-tube quick-disconnect with integral push in fittings	www.twintecinc.com	BC Series
30	Tank cleaning nozzle; BETE HydroWhirl Orbitor	www.bete.com	
31	Air impact wrench with speed control	www.globalindustrial.com	AirCat 803–RW 3/8" reactionless ratchet

INDEX

ReducedEffort® procedure, sustain, 147–149
Respect, 1, 5, 97, 107, 149, 151, 155–156
Retests process, for REC event, 90–98
Rockwell Automation, 16
Ruth, Babe, 159

S
Satterfield, Fred, 24–25
Saunders, Clarence, 151–153
Scheduling, REC event, 41, 43–46
Shingo, Shigeo, 3, 6, 27
Shingo, Ritsuo, 27, 28
Single Minute (or digit) Exchange of Dies (SMED), 15, 35–37, 39, 105
  definition of, 5
  development of, 3–4
  vs. ReducedEffort® Changeover events, 5–6
Six Sigma, 28
SOPs, *see* Standard operating procedures (SOPs)
Spaghetti Diagram, 49, 51, 53, 58–59, 70, 78, 94, 97–98, 124, 140
Spaghetti maker(s), 52, 53, 54, 58–59, 70, 91, 92, 94, 96, 97, 113, 124, 137, 140
Standard operating procedures (SOPs), 7, 10, 40, 44, 84–98, 108, 131, 136, 143, 147–149
Super Sticky Post-Its®, 48
Supply chain, 26–28, 32

T
Task Poster, 48, 52, 53–58, 114, 117, 120
Tasks
  choreographing, 73–77
  operators performance, 9–10
  poster, 53, 57–58
  writers, 53–56
Task Writer(s), 53–58, 65, 114, 117, 120–122

Team members, 92
Telegram, 11
Testing process, REC event, 90–98
Thread Wrap Coating, 158, 160
Timekeeper, 91, 92, 96
Timeline-building process, for REC event, 77–90
Tools, 99–106
Toyota Manufacturing Company, 4, 28, 30, 69–70
Toyota Production System (TPS), 5, 21, 28
Trashed tasks, 69, 76
Trial and error method, 7, 24

U
Upstream control, 27
Uptime tasks, standard operating procedures, 76, 77, 89–91, 131

V
Video-recordings, REC event, 9, 36, 37, 40–45, 47, 49, 51, 52–62, 66–67, 69–70, 72, 78–79, 82, 90–91, 94–95, 98–99, 109, 116–117, 124, 128–129, 136–138, 144

W
Walk to tasks, 75, 76, 81, 83
Wall of trash, 69
Watching process, REC event, 51–61
Watson, Thomas J., 160
Western Union, 11
Workers
  lean mentality, 28
  performance, 7–8
World class manufacturing, 19, 27, 32

Z
Zero defects, lean approach, 23–28
Zirkle, Mitch, 32–33

THE GREATEST LEADER IS THE GREATEST SERVANT

The greatest among you will be your servant. For whoever exalts himself will be humbled, and whoever humbles himself will be exalted.

—Mathew 23:11-12 (NIV)

ABOUT THE AUTHOR

Ron Heiskell has a BS in mechanical engineering and an MBA in technology management. A knowledgeable advocate and practitioner of Lean principles, Ron first developed and tested the Lean-driven process that evolved into the ReducedEffort system at The Clorox Company, where he was an engineer for 24 years.

During his first 22 years at The Clorox Company, Ron worked in the Machine Development Group, designing and building packaging machines and lines. During that time, he began teaching a class on product innovation at two California universities. As part of this class, he taught the role that paradigms play in people resisting new ideas. He also discovered a way to shift a person's paradigm very quickly.

When Ron was asked to teach SMED at The Clorox Company manufacturing plants, he agreed—in part because he saw it as his chance to try some new techniques. He knew that line workers had their own ways of performing changeovers and that many of them had been doing it the same way for a long time, often for 25 or more years. Their paradigms were well established. The challenge was to get them to readily shift paradigms and try something different. Teaching SMED at The Clorox Company gave Ron the opportunity to try this new reduced-effort process in the real world. The results were so amazing that his job shifted from designing packaging lines to reducing changeover downtime in all the plants owned by The Clorox Company as well as those of its suppliers.

After leaving The Clorox Company, Ron founded ReducedEffort, LLC., a company devoted to reducing changeover downtime. Since that time, he has been conducting ReducedEffort Kaizen Events at Fortune 500 companies throughout the United States and Canada.

Ron has received over fifty U.S. and foreign patents. He is the recipient of the AmeriStar Award from the Institute of Packaging Professionals, the Technology of the Year Award from *Packaging Technology & Engineering Magazine*, and the Dupont Award for Innovation.

9780367408909